FROM UNCERTAINTY OF IGNORANCE TO UNCERTAINTY OF SCIENCE

TRACTATUS SCIENTIFICO-PHILOSOPHICUS

ALEXANDER A. YABROV
MD, PhD, DSc

Author is a Laureate of the Best Book of the Year in Health Area award
(Awarded by the American Publishers Association)

ISBN: 0-7596-9297-1

This book is printed on acid free paper.

1stBooks - rev. 07/26/02

Dedication

In appreciation of the noble efforts of all those who contributed to the treasury of human knowledge from the prehistoric to modern times.

"Two approaches may be used in writing a book. In one, the author critically and objectively presents all data pertinent to the subject. This is the method of reporting presently used in the Western scientific community. In the other method, however, the author expresses his own views and analyses data. Several great writers, philosophers, and thinkers successfully followed this approach. Plato, Aristoteles, Kant, Marx, and Virchow are examples. The author chose the second approach.

Scientific knowledge is expanding geometrically helped along greatly by such minds as that of this author. The interpretations of the author may prove to be so appealing to his followers that knowledge about the subject will be pushed ahead by centuries."

Annals of Internal Medicine

Foreword

It has become unfashionable in medicine and in philosophy to ask the deepest questions about the existence of humans and the existence of the natural environment in its broadest sense. People who do ask such questions and who try to answer them are often dismissed as irrelevant to the very practical and materialistic concerns which dominate our current lives. Nothing could be further from the truth. These are among the most important questions of all and if we do not try to struggle with them, however vainly, we as a species will be less than we might be. We will also be much more likely to make appalling mistakes in the ways in which we deal with each other and with the natural world.

Alexander Yabrov is a highly unusual doctor, scientist and philosopher. On the one hand he is struggling in a very direct way to solve the practical problems of treating cancer. On the other, drawing strength from his profound knowledge of medicine, biology and the natural world, he is also trying to provide a broad philosophical framework for our existence and for our interactions with the natural world.

I was introduced to Dr Yabrov by the philosopher of science, Sir Karl Popper. Sir Karl was of the view that Dr Yabrov was an outstanding scientist and exceptional thinker. Sir Karl was right and over the twenty or more years during which I have been familiar with what Dr Yabrov is doing I have always been grateful to Sir Karl for that Introduction.

Dr Yabrov's book title is deliberate. At the beginning of the 21st century he is trying to do what Wittgenstein partially achieved in a different field in the early years of the 20th. He is trying to present a new worldview, which deserves the serious attention of all who are concerned about the future of humanity. His ideas deserve deep study and active implementation.

Professor David F. Horrobin.
Stirling, Scotland: November, 2001

From the Author

Influenced by the literature popularizing science, we are used to thinking that the interesting and unknown remains only somewhere beyond our planet. If we are interested in reading about the new discoveries concerning life on Earth, we are presented primarily with the findings of the creatures of the past, like dinosaurs, or the humanoids, which lived millions of years ago. When it comes to our time, it is believed that we would understand ourselves by studying behavior of the other species of animals, e.g., ants, dolphins, or chimpanzees.

This book proposes a fundamentally different approach that is an exact opposite to the well-established views about the world in which we live and what is considered worthy of a scientific–philosophical study. The central subject of our study is **us** – the modern men and women, and **our** world.

My professional experience as a physician and a cell biologist has taught me to consider the objects of my study *directly*. I believe that to understand ourselves, we should study ourselves – our health, our behavior, and our relationships. The object of my study is the modern individual with his everyday problems, needs, aspirations and concerns, rather than the populations or faceless masses.

The same direct approach is used in this book for the study of our environment. To study the world in which we live we separated *Our World* (limited by the solar system, but primarily – the earthly one) from the Universe. Such a division is warranted, because *our* world is the one of Order, which is based upon and manifested by the *existence* of natural objects. I summarise that Existence is the central subject of my study. Its aim is to understand and explain how *we* exist.

A.Y., Princeton, September 2001.

Unplanned addition, September 12, 2001

The proposition 12.5.6, the last in this book, was written at 6 p.m., September 10th, 2001. Next day, a picture of the terrorist attack against the United States was transmitted on TV at 9 a.m. On the same day, the President declared war against terrorism throughout the World.

Our World is not an abstract notion – it is the very *place* of our existence.

Existence is not an abstract notion – it is the *fact* itself that we exist.

How we exist - depends on *us*.

"Tractatus Scientifico-Philosophicus" and the *"How Man Exists"* are the first scientific studies of the *Existence*. For the first time, the reader meets the

ix

ideas of *Our* world, of Existence of Man and other natural objects – animate and inanimate, and of the influence of knowledge on our behavior and relationships – all considered from the *scientific* point of view.

As long as Man has existed, the problems of Existence (Being) have been considered from *religious* and *philosophical* points of view. But the scientific approach is necessary since only science *explains "How"*. This is achieved through discovery of the underlying *processes* and *mechanisms*. Understanding *"How"* man and other natural objects, and the World as a whole exist, gives us a broad vision. When this vision becomes widespread, it helps us to understand the others and ourselves. It is a *scientifically substantiated* truth that the laws of existence described in this book are valid for each and every one of us. When this truth is understood, it becomes obvious that the ideas, which divide the humankind now, contradict the basics of human relationships.

A.Y.

Call to Action, October 10, 2001

Among the first measures of national importance, President established an Office of Homeland Security. Governor of the State of Pennsylvania Mr. Tom Ridge was appointed an Office Director. Inauguration of Tom Ridge took place at the White House October 8th 2001 at Columbus Day. An official starting date of work of the Office was October 9th 2001. Next day – October 10/01 – I have received a personal telephone call from Mr. Tom Ridge. Conversation lasted about 30 minutes. Governor did most of the talking. He told me that he liked my Bioresistance Project and agreed that it should be a long-term project. We also discussed the central concept of the project, which Governor supported. Mr. Ridge told that this was an initial discussion and that I will be invited to Washington for a detailed talk with some experts.

Very briefly, I will describe the idea of my Project. A conventional approach is to look for the separate mechanisms of protection of the organism against particular injuring factors. The search is directed according to our professional or other narrow interests. For example, a search might be for the mechanisms of resistance to radiation, or to some chemicals, or to a certain bacterial agent. But the cells of the human organism do not have mechanisms according to every particular interest of an investigator. A cell has the mechanisms of resistance. I found that these mechanisms protect certain functions-structures that are *vital* for the cell. These are the mechanisms protecting structure of DNA, protein synthesis, transport, and production of energy. I named this group of mechanisms – the *mechanisms of security* (Yabrov, 1980). Study of these and similar mechanisms should result in the new methods of prevention and treatment of injuries caused by different agents. Thus we should search for the defence mechanisms not by our particular interests, but *by the vital interests of the cells.*

The reader might wonder that the Bioresistance Project and the *Tractatus Scientifico-Philosoficus* tackle seemingly absolutely disparate areas of problems. Explanation should be helpful for your further reading. Man is the most complex natural object. It comprises different basic levels of organization. Processes and mechanisms acting at these levels are different. However, existence of the organism as a whole is governed by a fundamental process common for all the levels. Understanding of this fundamental process of existence, which I name the process of *adequate functioning*, allows us to understand how man exists. Bioresistance Project studies adequate functioning at the subcellular-cellular and the organ-system levels of existence of man. *Tractatus* studies human behavior and human relationships that are the manifestations of the same fundamental process at the highest level of organization of man – the social level.

P.S. A month has passed after the September attack. Many questions were asked on the radio, television, and in the press. The officials, clerics, and the specialists of various kinds gave different answers. I have examined this book again. I did not add or deleted anything.

Man exists by the laws of nature independently of whether or not these laws are known. However, if he knows them, Man acts more efficiently in solving his problems. This was proven by our success in technology based on the knowledge of the laws of Motion. A scientifico-philosophical work describing the laws of Existence should not need updating as it concerns Existence of Man.

A.Y., Princeton, October 2001.

Content

Part Three: Influence of Common General Knowledge on Behavior of the Individuals and on Human Social Relationships

Part one:

Acquaintance

Alexander A. Yabrov, MD, PhD, DSc

Chapter 1.

Introduction

A world-recognised thinker of the 20s – Ludwig Wittgenstein published a book Tractatus –Logico-Phgilosophicus (1921), which puzzles the readers till today. Wittgenstein claimed that he observed a new phenomenon of great importance for mankind. But **what** he observed, he could not describe. Volumes were written about Wittgenstein's Tractatus, still the mystery remained.

My studies are centred on the natural phenomena of Existence. Comparative analysis of my long-term observations and of the works of the ancient and the modern philosophers led me, among other things, to the definitive conclusion that Wittgenstein observed the phenomena of **Existence**. He realised that he saw something *dissimilar* to the things studied by others, but he could not differentiate it by way of determining the features specific for the newly observed phenomenon. Having no specific characteristics, he could not name them and therefore could not describe *what* he observed.

The notion and the phenomena of Existence are described by me in the work *How Man Exists* (2001). I study existence *scientifically*, rather then philosophically. Therefore the work is not limited by the discovery of pertinent notions, but develops a scientific theory discovering also the processes and the mechanisms involved, and thus *explaining* How existence takes place.

New knowledge begets new questions that demand answers. Unexpectedly, I found myself in a situation similar to that of Wittgenstein. Based on the general understanding of existence I could see the **cause** of the current socio-cultural decay that increasingly destroys the very foundation of existence of man and the humankind. Spiritual degradation tremendously concerns everybody. Many eloquent descriptions of disturbing facts are published. But their general cause remains unknown. It is impossible to develop an effective program of remedial measures without knowledge of the fundamental cause of a problem.

To convey my new message, I had to pass through the consecutive stages of discovery, which also confronted Wittgenstein. Namely, to differentiate the specific features of the observed, to introduce new notions describing it and designate it by a certain term. In other words, to name the new phenomenon. These steps should have allowed me to overcome the barrier that prevented Wittgenstein from describing to the others what he saw. For a *scientific* study, however, these steps are necessary but insufficient. After passing them, I had to *explain how* the phenomena under consideration occur. This is what *this* book is about. After reading, it should become clear that the central topic of this study is the influence of *knowledge* on our behavior and relationships. Whether at all and how efficiently I conveyed my message is for the reader to judge.

Format of the presentation

Material is organised in the format used by Wittgenstein in his *Tractatus Logico-Philosophicus.*

In chapters 3 to 12, the ideas are presented as separate propositions. This allows the reader to focus attention on a certain idea disclosed in the proposition without loosing the overall thread of the study.

Each proposition contains an independent idea. At the same time, several consecutive propositions may belong to a common theme.

All propositions are marked by the 3-figure numbers. The first figure designates the chapter; the second – a common theme; and the third – the proper number of the proposition belonging to the same theme. Different themes are designated by the sub-titles.

The book is brief. This is an essential feature of my plan of the presentation. I find it necessary to discuss it with the reader. *Existence* is a one of the *eternal* problems occupying human thought. I approached this problem from a new position – the *scientific* one. A general scientific Theory of Existence is described in my previous book – *How Man Exists.* The fact of having a theory of existence does not *solve* the problem of existence, which is eternal. Rather following a new approach based on a scientific theory, we may consider effectively, understand and find solutions of particular problems of existence, many of which need an urgent solution. Aim of this *Tractatus* is to prove that the Evolutionary-Mechanistic worldview guiding us currently is socially destructive and therefore should be replaced by a new worldview – the Worldview of Existence. Attempts to present the theory of existence in more detail, or touch upon other existential problems would dilute the presentation and divert attention of the reader. Therefore many questions, which the reader might find important, are not discussed in this book. Some problems, though included, are not analyzed in detail. (Some of these problems are discussed at length in *How Man Exists*).

Chapter 2.

Why this Book is Named *Tractatus Scientiphico-Philosophicus*.

The exciting creative atmosphere of thoughts at the start of the 20th century

I invite the reader to trace with me the development of creative ideas at the start of the 20th century. This was a time of triumph of atomic physics. Below I give a very cursory list of discoveries.

Max Planck formulated Quantum Theory and published the "Laws of Radiation"(1900-1901). Albert Einstein formulated Special Theory of Relativity. At that time (1905), Einstein was an unknown technical clerk of the Swiss Patent Office. His absolutely new theory was hard to understand. (*The Times* of London characterized it as "an affront to common sense"). Yet, Planck, who was the editor of the *Annalen der Physik*, published Einstein's paper, which revolutionized our view of physical phenomena. Niels Bohr wrote on this occasion that Einstein and science were fortunate that the reviewer of the new theory happened to be Planck, because any other editor would have thrown the article into a paper basket. Soon after, Marie Curie published "Treatise on Radiography" (1910). Rutherford formulated his Theory of Atomic Structure (1911). J.J.Thomson published his "Rays of Positive Electricity and Their Application to Chemical Analysis" (1913).

Take a breath. We are approaching 1915 – the year when Einstein postulated his "General Theory of Relativity". The pace of discoveries increased further. Sir Arthur Eddington published "Gravitation and the Principle of Relativity" (1918). The validity of Einstein's theory was proven as a result of the total eclipse of the sun (1919). The same year, Rutherford demonstrated that the atom was **not** the *final* building-block of the universe. Next year, Sir Arthur Eddington published his "Space, Time, and Gravitation" (1920).

The aim of my very sketchy listing of the leading scientific studies at the beginning of the passed century is to illustrate that the ideas of quantum physics dominated the development of thought. Their influence spread upon the general public. The atmosphere of creative excitement was aggravated by the stir of the newspapers. Names of the physicists and the simplified descriptions of their discoveries occupied the first pages. The notions originated as a result of modern physical studies, such as *relativity* and also the principle of *uncertainty,* were transformed into *general* notions of relativism, and uncertainty or indeterminsm, applied for the description and understanding of all natural phenomena. Including those of our every day life, in particular of the human relationships. These

5

notions originating from quantum mechanics are currently forming our worldview, i.e., our common understanding of the world.

Interestingly, the aura of glamour associated with everything related to quantum physics remains. I had the opportunity to feel it every time when those who spoke with me learned that I was a Senior Scientist of the *Nuclear Physics Institute of the Academy of Sciences.* (Though I was a biologist, and studied how the human cells behaved under various conditions – favorable or unfavorable).

A mystery

Let us return to the beginning of the 20th century. In 1921, amid the intensive discussions of a general meaning of the new discoveries in quantum physics, a schoolteacher of mathematics, German philosopher Ludwig Wittgenstein (1889-1951) published a book - *Tractatus Logico-Philosophicus.* This event of the Western intellectual life did not pass unnoticed. Moreover, Wittgenstein's *Tractatus* does not cease to fascinate and intrigue the thinking readers throughout the world. Wittgenstein is now renowned as the leading analytical thinker of the 20th century.

The *Tractatus* did not discover and did not explain any new physical phenomena. It did not bring clarity in our understanding of nature and us. On the contrary: it ignited a *doubt*. Exactly this - the doubt – attracted an intense interest of the public.

Wittgenstein claimed that he observed something different and very important that others have not observed. On Wittgenstein's opinion, it was so essential that he considered this to be a "central problem of philosophy".

A puzzle was reinforced by that the author could not describe **what** he observed. Wittgenstein wrote in his *Tractatus*:

"There are, indeed, things that cannot be put into words. They *make themselves manifest.* They are what is mystical" (6.522). (Wittgenstein's emphasis. Here and further, figures in brackets – numbers of the propositions from the *Tractatus Logico-Philosophicus* (Routlege & Kegan Paul, London, 1974).

Many volumes have been written about the Wittgenstein's *Tractatus*. The mystery, however, remains unsolved. What Wittgenstein observed is not known. (For the reasons discussed in the first chapter, I find it not needed to analyse Wittgenstein's treatise in more details).

An answer to the question posed in the title of this chapter

We discussed briefly the circumstances under which the *Tractatus Logico-Philosophicus* was published and attracted the attention of the reader to its mystical message. Now I should answer the question posed in the title of this chapter. This will need a brief review of my studies.

By my educational background, I am a physician, medical virologist, and cell biologist. As a result of my professional experience and knowledge accumulated during twenty five years of clinical and experimental work, in the late 1970s, I naturally came to a stage of generalisation of my observations and thoughts.

My work was known among virologists, in particular those studying interferon - a natural protective protein produced in the human body. Still I remained essentially unknown in the West. I presented a compendium of my ideas to Sir Karl Popper – a leading thinker in the field of science, particularly biology. Sir Karl introduced me to Dr. David Horrobin, editor of the international scientific journal *Medical Hypotheses*. Dr. Horrobin advised me to send my materials to his Journal. The development of my studies since that time has been closely interrelated with this uniquely innovative scientific Journal.

The first article of a general character: "Maintenance of Adequate Function is a General Principle of Survival of Organisms" was published in 1979. It explained how every organism exists – by functioning adequately to needs. Thus the article for the first time defined and explained an *independent area* of biology – that of *existence of individual organisms* (in difference from that of the *origin of species* described by Darwin). This is a principal difference. Darwin explained how organisms originated - via the process of evolution. Evolutionary theory allowed us to understand an origin of the diverse forms of life. This knowledge is used in practice, especially in agriculture. But the knowledge of how a certain species originated does not help us to understand how every individual organism of this species exists. For example, thanks to the theory of evolution, we know how our species – Homo Sapiens – *originated*. But the evolutionary theory does **not** tell us how a person – you and I- *exists*. Though the evolutionary theory is *correct*, it **cannot** explain how we and other organisms exist, because not evolution but a different process is responsible for existence. This is the process of Adequate Function (synonym - Adequate Functioning).

The next general article: "Adequate Function of the Cell: Interaction Between the Needs of the Cell and the Needs of the Organism" (1980) – considered existence of a human organism at the cellular level. Later, it served as a basis of a new Theory of Pathology (2001).

Pertinent problems were discussed in my book *Interferon and Nonspecific Resistance* (1980).

Then followed a series of articles centred on a new task facing contemporary Medicine – <u>control over chronic diseases</u>: "New Trend in Medicine in the Developed Countries" (1985), "Medicine in the Long-Living Society" (1986), and "Reorganisation of Contemporary Medical Practice" (1986).

Besides the generalising ones, I published also the specialised papers on the problems of immunity, interferon, brain development, mechanisms of longevity and death, and also on AIDS. The last work might represent an interest for the general reader.

I did not have the opportunity to do an experimental work with the new disease. Being a virologist, I intently studied all pertinent publications. The first drug was invented – AZT. The tone of the publications was very optimistic. What puzzled me, however, that in spite of the sharp drop of the amount of the virus in the body, the treated patients still died, just as those who did not receive antiviral treatment. Thus the *antiviral* treatment did not prevent death. I did not question the role of the HIV virus in the initiation of the disease. But I suggested that <u>death</u> of the infected person was not caused by the virus. But rather by some different – non-multiplying factor, produced in the course of development of the disease, being triggered by the virus. I suggested that this factor could be an abnormally produced interferon. Among my recommendations was to treat the disease at an early stage – <u>before</u> its conversion from the asymptomatic sero-positive stage into the symptomatic AIDS stage (At that time, only the patients with the symptoms of a far advanced disease received antiviral treatment). This hypothesis I published in two consecutive papers in the *AIDS Research* (1986) and the *Medical Hypotheses* (1988). Recently, I have published an article: "It is Hazardous to Treat HIV-infected Patients with Interferon Alfa" (2000).

The following intensive studies confirmed my suggestions. It was shown that though AIDS was a viral disease, it primarily was a disease caused by severe distortion of function of the immune system. Dysregulated production of interferon was shown to be among the leading mechanisms and manifestations of the dysfunction of immune system in AIDS patients. Early use of the antiviral drugs became a standard method of treatment of AIDS.

Existence – a revelation

These works did not interfere with my studies of a more general character, which unexpectedly led me to the conclusion that the discovered by me principle of adequate function, which I initially qualified as the principle of survival of organisms, was <u>*valid* not only for the *living* creatures, but also for the *inanimate* natural objects</u>. From that moment (literally – there was such a moment of discovery – a revelation), I realised clearly that I moved from the area of research limited by medicine and biology, into the broadest possible sphere of natural phenomena – that of EXISTENCE.

I actualised the truth that all natural objects **do** *exist*. It might seem trivial. But this is the peculiarity of the laws of nature that you deal with the things, which everybody observes, so a discovery of some truth about these things may look trivial. I imagined the World around me in its completeness as follows.

A new law of nature

Our world is composed of *existing* objects. Existence of natural objects is manifested and described by the three general notions – *origin, motion* and *existence*. We will return to these notions in the following chapters. Here I emphasise that the above description allows me to differentiate phenomena of existence from *other* natural phenomena that we observe and understand – those of origin and motion. Furthermore, based on the results obtained initially with the living organisms, I could explain *how* existence takes place. It occurs via functioning – *adequate functioning*.

I had formulated my ideas in an article "General Principle of Existence of Natural Objects" (1986). It said that objects existed by functioning adequately to needs directed to the maintenance of their entity. Since a regularity characteristic both for the animate and inanimate natural objects was discovered, I classified it as a law of nature. (You will see from further analysis that this actually is a one of the laws of existence of Man and other natural objects).

Existence remained unexplained

The areas of phenomena of origin and of motion are explained by their fundamental theories – those of mechanics (classical and quantum) and evolution. I realized that the new sphere of natural phenomena needs to be explained by a corresponding general scientific theory – the Theory of Existence.

In order to free myself from the narrow topics, I summarised my ideas in the area of medicine in two articles: "General Mechanism of Chronic Diseases" and "Theory of Adequate Function of the Organism – the Theoretical Basis for Contemporary Medicine," both published in 1987. Since then I have devoted my work exclusively to the general theory of existence.

An original scientific study starts from a thorough research of the pertinent literature. For me, this was a period of self-education on the problem of Existence. I found **no** *scientific* studies of Existence. But a closely related area, embraced by the notion of Being, has been studied *philosophically* by religion and natural philosophy for millennia. In chapter 8, I will give the definitions, which reflect the commonality and the difference between these notions.

Among those who developed metaphysics – the study of Being - were the ancient Greeks – Parmenides, Plato, Aristotle, then in the middle ages – St. Thomas Aquinas, and in the modern time – Spinoza, Leibniz, and Kant. In the 20th century, guided by the evolutionary-mechanistic worldview, philosophy turned metaphysics into a target of severe criticism. *Being* is considered now as a nonsensical notion by most philosophers.

Heidegger was a lonely colossus, who dared to name Being the central problem of philosophy. In his *Being and Time* (1927), he repeated the question posed by Aristotle: "What is Being?" By his own utterance, Heidegger did not answer the question, but prepared the ground for the answer.

In the course of my search, the work by Wittgenstein – *Tractatus Logico-Philosophicus* (1921) attracted my attention. What did this thinker see that was so important that he contemplated suicide after being unable to describe his observations?

Results of my own studies and the comparative analysis of the works of the ancient and modern philosophers led me to a definitive conclusion that Wittgenstein observed **Existence**. It was, however insufficient to *see* a new phenomenon. It was necessary to differentiate it from the phenomena that were known, define it, and give it a name that bears a new notion. On my opinion, Wittgenstein could not convey his message because his thinking was limited by his mechanistic worldview. In the following chapters we will discuss the influence of a worldview on our thoughts, and our behavior and relationships. Thus Wittgenstein did not *describe* Existence, but he *observed* it. It is reasonable to suggest that the Wittgenstein's *Tractatus provoked* Heidegger.

I had not read the works of Wittgenstein and Heidegger prior to my literary search on the problem of Existence. But their ideas *were* in the treasury of human knowledge. They influenced the general thoughts about the World and about Man. This influence shaped my ideas, I believe. This is how knowledge develops – leaning on the shoulders of giants.

After finishing my description of the General Theory of Existence, I proceeded immediately to my work on the book, which I offer now to your attention. I decided to name it *Tractatus Scientifico-Philosophicus* as a tribute to Wittgenstein who so painfully and mystically touched upon the problem of Existence in his *Tractatus Logico-Philosophicus*.

The Tasks of this Book.

My previous book – *How Man Exists* (1ˢᵗ Library Books, 2001), describes the Theory of Existence, the Laws of Existence, and their applications. The applications include the practical areas, such as physiology and medicine, biotechnology, biology of existence of individual organisms, and the social sciences. They also embrace the area of general considerations, such as some problems of philosophy and science, and the problems of metaphysics.

The tasks of the Tractatus Scientifico-Philosophicus are the following.

- To substantiate the notion of *Our* World differing from that of the Universe.
- To develop a notion of a Worldview – a prevalent general idea shared by the majority about the World in which we live.
- To define the currently dominant worldview as the evolutionary-mechanistic one.
- To substantiate the destructive influence of the current worldview upon human relationships.
- To introduce a new worldview – the Worldview of Existence.
- To develop a new Theory of Human Relationships.

The ultimate goal of this *Tractatus* is to present a scientifico-philosophical justification for the **change of our worldview** from the evolutionary–mechanistic one to that of Existence. Human relationships are guided by ideas. The new understanding should help to stop and reverse the process of social degradation that threatens the very existence of man. A new worldview should help men in their efforts to improve the conditions of existence.

Alexander A. Yabrov, MD, PhD, DSc

Part Two:

The Modern Thought

Alexander A. Yabrov, MD, PhD, DSc

Chapter 3.

Uncertainty is a Guiding Idea of Modern Thoughts

3.1.1   The cave man's uncertainty was caused by ignorance.

3.1.2   Uncertainty of the modern man is based on science.

3.1.3   Uncertainty was not always a dominant idea. With growth of knowledge, the confidence grew. Its development was promoted by modern science at the dawn of it by the discoveries of Copernicus, Galileo and other thinkers. The idea of Order in Nature reached its zenith in the Cartesian mechanistic philosophy substantiated by the Newtonian mechanics.

3.1.4   In the 19th century, an idea of a permanent change of terrestrial objects, animate and inanimate, gradually took possession of the minds. It found its scientific substantiation in the works of Lamarck and Lyell and acquired its comprehensive formulation in Darwin's evolutionary theory. At the end of the century, the solid ground of classical physics started to shudder.   Doubts were triggered by the discovery of radioactive elements. Soon the ideas of atomic physics conquered the leading position in the formation of the views of the physicists. During the first quarter of the 20th century, determinism lost the remnants of its influence. In 1928, Heisenberg formulated his principle of uncertainty. A new worldview had been formed—the evolutionary-mechanistic one – the worldview of *uncertainty*. Absence of a cause, chance, statistical probability, indeterminism, continuous change and tendency to increasing chaos – these ideas became the leading ones not only in the area of the physics of particles, but also in consideration of *any* natural phenomena.

3.1.5   Wittgenstein, who had a physical education, reflected these modern views in his *Tractatus*. He said:

> "It is an hypothesis that the sun will rise tomorrow: and this means that we do not *know* whether it will rise" (6.3631).
> "There is no a priory order in things" (5.634).
> "There is no compulsion making one thing happen because another has happened" (6.37).

Wittgenstein rejects causality.

> "If there were a law of causality, it might be put in the following way: There are laws of nature. But of course that cannot be said: it makes itself manifest" (6.36).
> "The whole modern conception of the world is founded on the illusion that so-called laws of nature are the explanations of natural phenomena" (6.371).

3.1.6 Einstein was one of the few dissenters against the worldview of uncertainty. He wrote:

> "...I am quite convinced that some one will eventually come up with a theory, whose objects, connected by laws, are not probabilities but considered facts, as was until recently taken for granted. I cannot, however, base this conviction on logical reasons, but can only produce my little finger as witness, that is I offer no authority which would be able to command any kind of respect outside of my own hand." (see R. W. Clark, p. 609, 1971)

Chapter 4.

From Becoming to Being – From Chaos to Order

4.1   Theory of Order

4.1.1   There is an Order in *Our* World.

4.1.2   Our **Theory of Order** is based on the following general concepts:

    a. <u>*Discrete*</u> consideration of **Our World** and the rest of the Universe.

    b. **Fundamental Notions** describing all phenomena of *our* world – Origin, Motion and Existence.

    c. Principle of **Structural-functional organization** of objects of *our* world.

4.1.3.   Consider the following utterance by Popper from his *The Aim of Science*:

> "Almost all regions of the universe are filled by chaotic radiation, and almost all the rest by matter in a similar chaotic state... If the picture of the world which modern science draws comes anywhere near to the truth...then the conditions obtained almost everywhere in the universe make the discovery of laws of the kind we are seeking...almost impossible." (Popper, p. 170, 1988)

> The point is that *our* **world** *differs* **decisively from the rest of the universe**. Our conditions are different. Furthermore, the matter *our* world composed of is essentially different. These facts led us to conclusion that *Our* World should be considered **discretely** from the rest of the universe. The laws we are seeking, those describing the earthly phenomena, in particular those related to life, could be found only in *our* world. They might be not valid for the rest of the universe and vice versa.

4.2   *Our* World

4.2.1   I emphasise that we consider not the cosmic phenomena, but those of *our* world.

4.2.2   The notion of *Our* World embraces primarily the earthly phenomena. Phenomena related to other planets within the solar system probably also belong here. But I concentrate on the earthly ones.

4.2.3   I prefer not to speculate whether the laws of *our* world are also valid for some *other* worlds where *existence* of natural objects is preserved (if there are such worlds).

4.3   Fundamental Notions

4.3.1.   All the natural phenomena of *our* world are described by the notions, or concepts of **Origin, Motion and Existence.**

4.3.2   My definition of a *natural phenomenon* includes an object, which occupies space, and what is going on with this object.

4.3.3   There are no phenomena beyond the notions of Origin, Motion and Existence. Therefore we name them – *fundamental notions.*

4.3.4   Fundamental notions allow us to recognise and to realise the Order in *our* world. If the major attribute of a phenomenon is considered, every phenomenon belongs to Origin, Existence and Motion, or to their combination.

4.3.5   The above notions in their interrelation can describe every object of nature in its major aspects. Each object has an origin, exists, and is in motion.

4.4   Time of Existence

4.4.1   The notion of *endless* Time is fundamental in our description of the Universe. But the Time of Existence of individual objects of *our* world is *finite*. This, first of all, refers to animate objects. Thus we introduce a specifically **earthly** notion of *Time* – a finite time of existence of a natural object. For example, a lifetime of a man.

4.4.2   I use the length of time of existence – duration, or longevity – as a characteristic of an adequate and inadequate functioning (see further – the laws of nature).

4.5   *Our* World – the world of existence

4.5.1   *Existence* of objects is what primarily differentiates *our* world from the rest of the universe. Earthly objects animate and inanimate tend to maintain their individuality and thus they exist as particular entities.

4.5.2   As a matter of fact, all the basic sciences study the manifestations of Existence. Physics and chemistry study how *existing* objects interact. Evolutionary geology and biology study how the *existing* objects originated. The sciences of existence, among them biology of existence of individual objects, physiology, medicine, and social sciences, study how the objects *exist*.

4.6   Another general concept

4.6.1   I started this chapter from statement that our Theory of Order is based on the three general concepts. Two of those – (1) discrete consideration of *our* world and (2) fundamental notions of Origin, Motion and Existence - have been discussed just above. The third general concept describing *order* in nature is the *Principle of structural-functional organization*.

4.6.2   Phenomena belonging to a certain fundamental notion, can be grouped by the *structures* of the objects involved.

For example, phenomena of Motion occur within two distinct structural groups: those of physical particles, atoms and molecules, and those of physical bodies.

All the phenomena of Origin occur in two distinct structural groups *different* from those of Motion. Thus when we consider the origin of terrestrial objects, we are dealing with the origin of geoformations (valleys, hills, mountains, and the like) - the inanimate objects; and with the origin of species of organisms - living objects.

When we consider the phenomena of Existence of individual natural objects, we discover to our surprise, that in spite of the endless diversity of objects, their *structural organization* is *common* to all objects. For example, the atomic-molecular structure is common to all objects, inanimate and animate. The cellular structure is common to all living objects.

These structural characteristics common to different objects I call the *structural levels* of organization.

4.6.3.   Understanding of a phenomenon emerges from posing questions *"What,"* and *"How"* - the major questions tackled by science.

By describing structure, we answered the *What*; we described the object involved in the phenomenon, which we observe and want to explain.

Knowledge of the structure of an object is necessary. However, it is insufficient for the understanding of a phenomenon. The next step towards understanding is the answer to the *How* – how a phenomenon occurs. As a matter of fact, we should answer <u>two</u> *Hows*, for we need to describe the *processes* <u>and</u> the *mechanisms* that underlay and govern the phenomenon under study.

4.7 Processes and mechanisms

4.7.1 Natural phenomena proceed according to certain *processes*. Discovery of an underlying process by which pertinent phenomena proceed is a key to the *understanding* of phenomena.

4.7.2 A process that underlies all the phenomena pertinent to a certain fundamental notion I call a *fundamental process.* Thus of the multiplicity of processes, there are three *fundamental* ones: *physical-chemical interactions, evolution* and *adequate functioning* underlying phenomena embraced by the notions of motion, origin and existence, correspondingly.

4.7.3 A process represents a sequence of certain steps, or changes, according to which a phenomenon develops. These consecutive steps, or changes, are provided by certain natural means, or tools, which I call *mechanisms*. For example, gravitation is the mechanism responsible for the interaction of physical bodies. Natural selection is one of the mechanisms of the origin of species. Instincts belong to the mechanisms of an organism's existence.

4.7.4 We have considered the structural levels, and the processes and the mechanisms (i.e., structure and function) - separately. In reality, however, these components are inseparable. Consider as an example a phenomenon from the area of Motion: a diving man. We observe the diver (*structure*) falling (*functioning*) – the function being represented by the *process* of interaction provided for by the *mechanism* of gravitation. Together, these components: structure *and* function, represent a phenomenon.

The inseparability of structure and function is also characteristic for the phenomena of Origin and Existence.

4.7.5 We thus should speak not of the structural, but the *structural-functional levels* of organization of natural objects.

4.7.6 The regularity of the interrelations of structure and function I call the *principle of structural-functional organization* of nature.

4.8 Consequences

4.8.1 *A hierarchy of the structural-functional levels of existence.* In a complex object, having several structural-functional levels, the higher level governs the activity of the lower ones. Thus in a man we differentiate the atomic-molecular, cellular, organ–system, organism-behavioral, and the social levels of organisation. The social level controls and governs the functions of the lower ones. For example, an individual participates in a mountain climbing competition – a social undertaking. Functions at all the levels – organism, organ-system, cellular and the sub-cellular -are subordinated in a consecutive order to the needs of the social level.

4.8.2   Conclusions obtained as a result of observations of the phenomena at a certain structural-functional level, *cannot* be applied automatically to all *other* levels of which an object is composed. Man is the most complex natural object. Conclusions pertaining to the atomic-molecular level are *inapplicable* for understanding of phenomena observed at the social one and vice versa, because *different mechanisms* are responsible for the phenomena at every level.

4.8.3   *Scope of a theory is determined by the process.* A scientific theory can explain only the phenomena underlain by a process discovered by this theory. Therefore, e.g., the theory of Origin, which discovered the process of evolution, **cannot** be applied for explanation of human relationships. Because the latter belong to the area of phenomena of Existence. Explanation of human relationships should be based on the theory of Existence, which discovered the process of existence – the process of *adequate functioning*. Hence the principle of appropriateness.

4.8.4   *The principle of appropriateness.* A scientific theory of a narrower scope should be based on an appropriate general theory describing corresponding *fundamental process.* Thus all the particular and basic theories tackling various phenomena of Motion should be based on the theory of mechanics. Most of those dealing with the phenomena of Origin should be based on the theory of evolution. Contrariwise, the theories tackling phenomena of Existence should be based on the theory of adequate functioning (a theory of existence).

4.8.5   The Theory of Existence was not known until today. Philosophers and scientists based their consideration of phenomena of existence on the theories of evolution and mechanics. Disregard of the principle of appropriateness inevitably led to erroneous recommendations. Marx's social theory is a notorious illustration.

4.9   Existence   and   Order   –   cardinal   inseparable characteristics of *our* world

4.9.1   The foundation of our Theory of Order is formed by the concepts of a discrete consideration of *our* world; of the fundamental notions; and of the structural-functional organization. At the same time, the concepts of fundamental notions and of structural-functional organization represent the foundation of our Theory of Existence (described in *How Man Exists*, 2001). Thus the theories of Order and of Existence *merge*.

4.9.2   This merger of the theories is a reflection of **reality** of *our* world. Existence of the natural objects, animate and inanimate, is the *basis* **and** the *manifestation* of Order. Existence of individual objects is what primarily differentiates *Our* World from the rest of the Universe.

4.9.3   At the same time, Existence of the individual objects maintaining their entity is impossible without Order in Nature.

4.9.4   We conclude - *Existence and Order are the two inseparable basic characteristics of our world.*

4.10   The laws of physics are <u>not the only</u> laws of nature

4.10.1   It follows from the above considerations that a profound <u>conflict</u> exists between some views *<u>about reality</u>* based on modern physics and the *<u>actual</u>* <u>reality</u> of *our* world. An utterance by Einstein is appropriate here: "The more success the quantum theory has, the sillier it looks" (Einstein, 1912). Paradoxically, we became used to this. We consider the physical laws as the *only* laws of nature. Consequently, we use the laws of physics for description of any phenomena of *our* world. However, the physical laws, though they are correct, in many cases do **not** reflect our every day reality. Consider the illustration below.

4.10.2   This is how Richard Feynman[1] analyses the distinction of past and future in his *The Character of Physical Law* (1990). He gives the following examples. We remember the past, we do not remember the future. If we take a movie picture showing various everyday phenomena and run the film backward, the viewers would laugh, because, in real life the events do not go back. The pieces of a broken cap do not move backward to reconstruct it. The physicist says then:

> "If the world of nature is made of atoms, and we too are made of atoms and obey physical laws, the…interpretation…would be that some of the motion laws of the atoms are going one way… But we have not found this yet. In all laws of physics that we have found so far there does not seem to be any distinction between past and future… If we take a moving picture of a planet going around the sun in some direction and run the moving picture backward…the

---

[1] Richard Feynman – recipient of the 1965 Nobel Prize in Physics for his studies in quantum electrodynamics.

physicist who looks at it should not laugh... The law of gravitation is of such a kind that the direction does not make any difference...(Feynman, pp. 108-109; 1990).

One more example from the same work by Feynman:

There is no model of the theory of gravitation...other than the mathematical form... Every one of our laws are purely mathematical... Why? I have not the slightest idea..., Feynman says (Ibid, p.39).

4.10.3   My explanations of the previous examples are based on the Theory of Existence. Phenomena of our every day life, e. g. our social activities (thinking, reading, bargaining, buying, selling, etc.), belong to the sphere of *Existence* **not** Motion. Laws of nature that are valid in each of these spheres are *different*. The laws of motion are reversible, but the laws of existence are not. *Every day phenomena* shown in a movie picture are **not** the *physical* phenomena. These are the events of *Existence. A*nd all the theorisation about the "motion laws of the atoms going one way..." suggested by the physicist are irrelevant to the situation under consideration. My point is that the "motion laws of the atoms" are **inapplicable for the description and explanation of the phenomena of Existence.** The phenomena of our every day life are considered and explained by the different laws of nature – Laws of Existence.

4.10.4   The laws of physics are mathematical because they operate by the notions, which are measurable and calculable (e.g., mass, speed, acceleration, and the like). The laws of existence are **not** mathematical because they operate by the *non*-measurable and *non*-calculable notions, such as adequate and inadequate functioning, needs, reason, morals, and the like. In other words, not *all* the laws of nature are mathematical.

4.11   What is a Law of Nature?

4.11.1   I define a law of nature as a certain regularity of a fundamental process. Physical laws describe regularities of the process of physical-chemical interactions, governing phenomena of Motion. There are still two other fundamental processes – those of evolution, and adequate functioning – governing phenomena of Origin and Existence, correspondingly. Consequently, the laws of Motion, are **not** the **only** laws of nature. We should consider also the laws of Origin, and of Existence (the Laws of Existence are considered in chapter 7).

4.11.2   In relation to the above, I should emphasise that the *Theory of Everything* (TOE), on which many physicists are currently working, is a general theory of *Motion*, but not of *everything*.

4.12   Conclusions and the laws of quantum physics valid for cosmic phenomena might be inappropriate for the phenomena of *Our* World

4.12.1   The conclusions obtained via cosmic studies, though correct, might be *inapplicable* for the general understanding of the phenomena of our every day life.

4.12.2   For example, it follows from the results obtained by Einstein that under the condition of speed nearing that of light some properties of the objects such as mass, size, and the functioning rate change. I attract your attention to the fact that the properties just mentioned could be considered as the <u>manifestations of *existence.*</u> I came to conclusion that at the super-speeds a new process takes place, which I categorise as the *existence-in-motion*. This process is not observed in *our* world. But in the cosmic universe some phenomena probably proceed by this process. From this point of view, Einstein's equation $E = mc2$ can be viewed as formulating the correlation of motion and existence at super-speeds.

4.12.3   Another example. It was found by Prigogine[2] that in the course of chaotic interaction of particles, a transient self-organisation of matter takes place. According to his theory of deterministic chaos, Prigogine suggested that self-organisation, taking place on a cosmic scale during endless time, could lead to formation of our solar system and the development of life. We deal with the gradual accumulation of changes occurring as a result of the interaction of particles in motion, therefore I characterise the process underlying phenomena of deterministic chaos as that of *evolution-in-motion*. It is possible that this process underlies certain cosmic phenomena.

4.12.4   There is an *essential difference* between the above cosmic processes and the fundamental processes acting in *our* world. In the cosmos, existence and motion are *interdependent.* We deal with a *new* process where motion immediately influences existence of an object.

---

[2] Ilya Prigogine – received the Nobel Prize for Chemistry in 1977 for contributions to nonequilibrium thermodynamics.

The same should be said about cosmic evolution expressed in the deterministic chaos. It *depends* and is *inseparable* from continuous motion of particles in large populations.

4.12.5   In *our* world the fundamental processes are *not* interdependent immediately. Motion does not influence manifestation of the phenomena of existence. If it did, the trackers, pilots and the "frequent flying" passengers would look appreciably younger and live longer than the other individuals. But this does not take place. Neither does Motion determine evolution. In *our* world, fundamental processes proceed *independently* from one another.

4.13   Clash of opinions helps discovery of new notions

4.13.1   In July of 1999, I visited Professor Prigogine to discuss the problem of Existence. I started from the assertion that the world is described by the notions of Motion, Origin and Existence. However, Dr. Prigogine's opinion was that the idea of the notion of Existence was superfluous—everything was described by the process of evolution of the moving particles. And this is how everything *existed*. No additional notion was necessary...

4.13.2   I was stunned. The necessity of the *notion* of Existence seemed so obvious to me that I lost my ability of persuasion. Dr. Prigogin was so kind that he took some reading material from me. Yet, our discussion the next day did not change anything. After I left the Institute, I did not notice how long and where was I roaming, speaking with myself in the foreign Brussels. Eventually, I regained consciousness and found a person who spoke English. It took me more than an hour *by the streetcar* to return to the center of the city. This fiasco inspired me to introduce and substantiate the concept of a *discrete consideration* of the *cosmic* world (considered by the theory of Deterministic Chaos) and of *our* world (considered by the theory of Order and the theory of Existence).

4.13.3   This previous point does not exclude the possibility that some phenomena of *our* world proceeded by the process of evolution-in-motion. Now it does not play the role of a *fundamental* process here, i.e., of a process that underlies phenomena at all the structural-functional levels. But it might, for example, play a role in some pathological phenomena at the sub-cellular level.

4.13.4   Thus it can be suggested that the connective tissue which envelopes all the cells and organs represents a semi-fluid whose particles are in nonequilibrious state (a situation explored in the Prigogine's models). During a sufficient time, some statistical processes of self-organization may manifest their role. For example, in the course of the development of an embryo, which is strictly controlled by specific mechanisms, a deviation might take place caused by the local formation of temporary structures resulting from the process of self-organization involving populations of suspended particles of the connective tissue. Transient self-organization is a major manifestation of the process of evolution-in-motion. This might explain some anatomical or genetic malformations in a new-born. For example, ectopic (located away from normal position) neural cells, which may cause epileptic seizures.

4.13.5 Similar considerations might also be applicable for the explanation of gradual changes accumulating in the course of ageing. It can be surmised, based on the theory of deterministic chaos, that the time-related changes in the connective tissue are the consequences of the processes of self-organization and of gradual transition from a nonequilibrious state toward the equilibrium. These changes, in their turn, influence the properties and vitality of the cells. Features common for an aged body, such as stiffness of joints, rigidity of vessels, fragility of bones, etc., may have a new explanation. This view might be broadened because other tissues may also be considered as particular liquids. The well known observations of the positive role of regular physical exercise and continuous mental activity might get a new consideration as the factors opposing the structural changes resulted from age-related self-organization.

I also hypothesised that by reproducing the process of existence-in-motion in earthly conditions, it would be possible to extend considerably the longevity of our technical equipment and even of human life (see *How Man Exists*, 2001).

4.14 In defence of causality

4.14.1 Not only the cosmic phenomena, but also those observed in *our* world at the sub-atomic level are used for the substantiation of the currently dominant worldview rejecting Order. *Negation of causality* and the *principle of uncertainty* are the pillars upon which the current worldview is based.

4.14.2 Generalised rejection of *causality* is based in particular on the observation of an electron relocating from a one orbit around the nucleus to the other without an established cause.

The following arguments, however, may testify against this all-embracing generalisation, which contradicts our everyday experience.

4.15   A history of negation

4.15.1 The initial attack against causality was undertaken by Hume in the 17th century. Hume asserted that it was impossible to prove that an event classified as the cause actually *induced* the one considered being its effect. No connection between the cause and effect was established but just the fact that a one phenomenon follows the other. Philosophers-rationalists including Kant, Hegel and recently Russell and Popper could not refute Hume's arguments. Negation of cause-and-effect relations resulted in the development of scepticism in regard to the reliability of our knowledge.

> "No theory of knowledge should attempt to explain why we are successful in our attempts to explain things. Hume's result established for good that all our universal laws or theories remain forever guesses, conjectures, hypotheses... This is Hume's negative solution of the problem of induction, a solution which I fully endorse", said Popper (p. 107; 1983).

And now we have a modern affirmation of Hume's claim in the example of an electron changing orbits seemingly without a cause.

4.15.2 But if we consider Hume's arguments based on contemporary knowledge, it becomes clear that it is *possible* to show the cause-and-effect relations in every example suggested by Hume in 1854 (consider collision of the billiard-balls, or relations of flame and heat) (see *How Man Exists*, 2001). Electron changes orbits of its motion without a known cause. It is hard to exclude a possibility that in 150 years from today the cause of the electron changing orbits will be discovered. On what ground will we base our general rejection of causality then?
Even if we proceed from the *current* knowledge, a general refutation of causality is not warranted, nor is the all-embracing scepticism in regard to our ability to explain things.

4.16   Our contra-arguments

4.16.1 We base our contra-arguments on the Theory of Existence and Order. According to the principle of appropriateness that follows from the concept of fundamental notions, a conclusion based on the observation limited to the area of Motion *cannot* be spread onto the phenomena of Existence. Even if we refer a subatomic phenomenon to the area of

Existence, another rule occurs to be violated – that of *difference* of the structural-functional levels of organization. A conclusion based on the facts observed only on a certain organizational level cannot be generalised on the *other* levels, because of the *difference of the mechanisms* involved. For example, mechanisms acting at the subatomic level are the forces of interaction, whereas mechanisms acting at the organism-behavioral level of existence are instincts and reflexes. When an electron changes orbits in an atom of a gazelle's body, we conclude that it occurs without a cause. When, however, this gazelle follows her instinct of self-preservation in trying to escape from a lion, we cannot generalise that there is no cause for her to ran because electrons in her body change orbits seemingly without a cause. The cause of her sudden ran is the attack of a predator.

4.16.2　The previous example belongs to the area of Existence. We may consider the levels of organization *within* the area of Motion. The same rule applies. Mechanisms acting at the level of physical particles are the electromagnetic, and the weak and strong forces of interaction. Considering phenomena of motion at *this* level, we speak of an absence of a cause and of the necessity to rely on the statistical probability. But we cannot generalise our conclusions on *all* the phenomena of motion. At the level of physical bodies, where the mechanism of interaction is *gravitation*, causality is acknowledged.

4.16.3　We come to the conclusion that the negation of causality can be applied only to the *motion of particles*. It cannot be considered as a *universal* principle.

4.17　Relativity of uncertainty

4.17.1　For centuries, physicists observed the motion of planets (and of other physical bodies) and they knew that observation itself did not influence the motion. When, however, they tried to look at an electron to study its motion, they discovered that observation itself influenced the results. The beam of light directed at the electron disturbed motion of the latter. Heisenberg was the first to discover that it was impossible to determine simultaneously the position and velocity of motion of an illuminated electron. Scientists and philosophers were so amazed and impressed that they generalised this particular observation to a *principle* of indeterminacy, or uncertainty. It follows from our theory that this *generalisation* is **not** warranted.

4.17.2　First of all, uncertainty refers to the phenomena of motion. It cannot be generalised on the phenomena of existence because *different fundamental processes* are involved – those of interactions and of adequate functioning, correspondingly (the principle of appropriateness). Secondly, it is observed *only* at a sub-atomic level. It cannot be generalised on other levels because different *mechanisms* are involved (principle of structural-functional organization).

4.18   Does uncertainty exist?

4.18.1   It can be suggested that the uncertainty does not exist *in reality*. Heisenberg *could not determine* the position and velocity of an electron simultaneously. But this does not mean that an electron *does not have* a certain position and velocity. Even if one assumes that an electron behaves like a wave (so that its position might be hazy), it still should have certain limits manifested by the stability of an existing object (e.g., the gazelle) composed of atoms and electrons.

4.18.2   Thus based on the Theories of Order and Existence we assert that the worldview of uncertainty does not reflect the reality of *our* world. Current *knowledge in its entirety* presents the worldview of the dominance of Order in *Our* World.

Alexander A. Yabrov, MD, PhD, DSc

Part Three:

Influence of Common General Knowledge on Behavior of the Individuals and on Human Social Relationships

Alexander A. Yabrov, MD, PhD, DSc

Chapter 5.

Knowledge

5.1 The sources of knowledge

5.1.1 General knowledge is a body of intelligence about the world.

5.1.2 Knowledge is obtained from different *sources*.

5.1.3 Among the primary sources of knowledge is the individual's ***Experience*** – personal and that learned from the others. Though very important, individual experience is inevitably limited and biased.

5.1.4 Individual experience is complemented, enriched and made objective by the knowledge obtained from the *general sources*. Among general sources of knowledge I differentiate ***Science, Philosophy, Religion, Technology*** *and* ***Art.***

5.1.5 As a source of knowledge, technology can be considered as a derivative *of science*.

5.1.6 As a source of knowledge, art can be considered as a derivative of *all other* sources of knowledge. By my definition, art represents the artist's view of the world based on individual experience enriched by knowledge from general sources expressed by the method of the artist's trade.

5.1.7 Thus *Science, Philosophy* and *Religion* are the ***major*** general sources of knowledge.

5.1.8 Each of the sources of knowledge brings information from different *areas* of natural phenomena obtained by different *methods*. Therefore it is important that **all** the sources be exploited and the information obtained from each source be combined with that from the others.

5.2 Dominance of modern science as the only general source of knowledge

5.2.1 Currently, the *scientific* knowledge overwhelmingly *dominates* the knowledge from other sources. This is especially characteristic of the Western culture.

5.2.2 Of the major general sources of knowledge, modern science is the youngest one.
Like a cuckoo, it *ousted* religion and natural philosophy, the sources from which it developed.

5.2.3 The dominance of science as a source of knowledge has consequences of a technological and social character.

5.2.4 From the *technological* point of view, prevalence of a scientific approach has a positive role in that it prefers more precise, experimentally proven information. Its beneficial influence manifested itself in a tremendous development of technology.

5.2.5 Regarding the *social* aspect, however, dominance of science at the expense of other sources of knowledge has a devastating effect because social existence of man ***cannot be understood*** without using **all** the sources of knowledge that humankind possesses.

Chapter 6.

Science

6.1 Definitions

6.1.1 Science is an intellectual activity aimed at discovery and explanation of natural phenomena.

6.1.2 To explain a phenomenon, it is necessary to discover the *process* by which it occurs and the *mechanisms* responsible for this process.

6.1.3 Knowledge of the underlying processes and mechanisms allows us to understand *how* a phenomenon occurs. Furthermore, it allows understanding how *other* pertinent phenomena occur.

6.1.4 Phenomena *are* interrelated, *because* they are underlain by a <u>common process.</u>

6.2 Role of the scientific theories

6.2.1 "What constitutes science – a fact, or a theory?" Most of the scientists, whom I asked, answered – "a fact". I disagree. Fact is merely information, though important. An apple fell from a tree – a fact, but <u>not</u> science. A theory of gravitation <u>is</u> science.

6.2.2 The scientific theories discover the processes and mechanisms that underlie natural phenomena.

6.2.3 We differentiate the *particular, basic* and the *fundamental* scientific theories by the breadth of the scope of phenomena they explain.

6.2.4 Particular theories are the ones which discover *particular processes* underlying a certain phenomenon, or a *limited* group of pertinent phenomena. Here belong the theories that consider and explain phenomena studied by various disciplines, specialities and sub-specialities. For example, various astronomical, chemical, or medical theories.

6.2.5 Basic theories discover the *basic processes*. They describe and explain all the phenomena, which belong to a certain basic structural-functional level of organization of nature. For example, the theories of classical and of quantum mechanics are different basic theories explaining all the phenomena governed by the processes of interaction of physical bodies or of interaction of physical particles, correspondingly. Contrariwise the theories of origin of the inanimate and of the animate terrestrial objects are the different basic ones explaining phenomena of evolution of geo-formations or of evolution of the species of organisms, correspondingly.

6.2.6 Explanation provided by the *fundamental* theories embrace the broadest possible areas of pertinent phenomena - those of Motion, Origin and Existence. These are phenomena underlain by the *fundamental processes* of interaction, evolution and adequate functioning, correspondingly.

6.3 A Theory of Existence

6.3.1 The process of adequate functioning underlies all the phenomena of *existence* taking place at different structural-functional levels comprising the individual natural objects. For example, man – the most complex object of nature – comprises the atomic-molecular, cellular, organ-system, organism-behavioral, and the social levels. The Theory of Existence discovered that all the phenomena pertinent to existence of man proceed by the process of adequate functioning. Furthermore, it was shown that phenomena of existence of *all* natural objects - animate and inanimate, occurring at any organisational level, proceed by the process of adequate functioning (see *How Man Exists*, 2001).

6.3.2 Theory of Existence (Theory of Adequate Functioning) discovered a fundamental process, i.e., the one underlying phenomena at all the levels, and described the mechanisms providing for this process at different levels. Therefore this theory should be classified as the *fundamental* one.

6.3.3 Following the above classification, the theories of classical mechanics, quantum mechanics, evolution of species, and of evolution of geo-formations should be considered as the *basic* ones.

6.3.4 Extensive studies are being performed currently aimed at development of a unified theory, which would explain all the phenomena belonging to the area of Motion (an idea suggested initially by Einstein). The example of the theory of existence confirms that, in principle, it is possible to develop a general theory explaining *all* the phenomena embraced by a one of the fundamental notions (by the notion of Existence, or by the notion of Motion, correspondingly).

6.3.5 For the purpose of this study, it is suggested that three fundamental theories be recognised. Those of Existence, Motion and Origin.

6.4 Neither the evolutionary theory, nor the theory of mechanics could explain the phenomena of existence

6.4.1　As I emphasised, a scientific theory can explain only those phenomena, which are governed by one and the same process discovered by this theory. This refers to all theories *including the fundamental* ones. In spite on their breadth, the latter theories are still limited in their explanatory capability by a process discovered by them. For example, the evolutionary theory is applicable *only* for the explanation of phenomena of Origin governed by the process of evolution. The theory of mechanics (classical and quantum) can be used *only* for the explanation of phenomena of Motion underlain by the process of interaction (of the physical bodies and particles). These two theories, separately or combined, *do not describe* and *cannot explain* phenomena of Existence of natural objects.

6.5 Certain level of general development of science was necessary for the Theory of Existence to be elaborated and introduced

6.5.1　One might wonder why the history of development of science would not take a different course? Why a scientific theory explaining <u>Existence</u> would not be introduced prior to those explaining Motion and Origin? This is an interesting question because the transformation of a worldview of Being directly into that of Existence with the appearance of modern science seems to be more natural.

6.5.2　The following answer may clarify the confusion. Religion and philosophy did not discover the processes and mechanisms of the natural phenomena, which they described. *How* the phenomena occurred remained unknown. Science developed as a consequence of a human quest for understanding of *How*. Long-term practice showed that the simplest way to find the answer to *How* was a direct experiment. The most amenable for experimental studies happened to be phenomena of Motion. Therefore phenomena of motion became the initial subject of scientific studies. New notions and theories, including the fundamental, appear only when the existing ones prove to be unable to solve certain problems. The science of Motion could not explain phenomena of Origin and of Existence. Phenomena of Origin proved to be more easily amenable to direct observation and comparative analysis at the level of development that science reached at the 19th century. Therefore the scientific theory of Origin appeared next.

6.5.3　The phenomena of Existence studied for millennia by religion and philosophy proved themselves to be the most difficult for a scientific study. Sciences of Motion and Origin deal with the populations (of particles, organisms etc.). This makes generalizations much easier than in the case of the science of Existence, whose central subject of consideration is an *individual* object. The amount of natural objects is enormous. Their diversity is tremendous. It is not feasible and it is practically useless to have theories explaining existence of every individual object separately.

6.5.4　Consider man as an example. Each person is unique. Individual theories of existence of every person would be useless because they could not be applicable for a general explanation of the relationships of all these individuals. A scientific study should necessarily lead to certain generalizations. Therefore the scientific theory of Existence appeared now - when science reached the level of development appropriate to the task.

6.6　Profession of a physician - the most appropriate for the development of a General Theory of Existence

6.6.1　I should like to add that of all the specialties, that of a physician is the most appropriate for the study of Existence as a notion independent of those of Motion and Origin. The Medical doctor bases investigations neither upon the theory of mechanics nor of the evolution of species. Rather a physician relies on the observation and analysis of the signs of health and disease, and bases his generalizations on a particular theory of medicine. In other words, physician scientifically studies phenomena of *existence,* his mind not being tainted by the ideas of motion or origin. The doctor, of course, knows about the theories of mechanics and evolution (and agrees with them), but does not rely on these theories while helping a patient to overcome a disease. I leave alone the arguments that the doctor might exploit some contrivances, or some methods of genetic investigations. But we discuss here a general theoretical base of medicine and conclude that it is not formed by the theories of mechanics and evolution.

6.6.2　This may seem very abstract. In reality, however, these considerations have an immediate *practical* relevance to understanding of the role of modern science in human relationships.

Chapter 7.
Science and Human Relationships

7.1 A notion of WORLDVIEW

7.1.1 Science exerts a tremendous influence on relationships of people and behavior of individuals *via* the *worldview*.

7.1.2 Every person has some opinion about the narrow world that encircles this individual. It includes the living conditions, the relationships with one's peers, the way of their behavior, and the like. This is a personal world view based on the knowledge resulted primarily from personal experience. It helps an individual to understand what is going on in one's neighbourhood, to foresee the immediate course of events, and to adjust one's behavior accordingly.

7.1.3 I introduce a much broader notion - that of a **WORLDVIEW** – a *general* understanding of the world we live in – i.e., of *our* world. Worldview is based on the currently dominating *general* knowledge accepted by the majority.

7.1.4. Worldview plays a grandiose role in human relationships.
The influence of worldview might be not realised consciously. This, however, does not negate its guiding role. *Man is guided by ideas*. Ideas are based on knowledge. This is what I emphasised at the beginning of our study – the guiding role of knowledge on the behavior of individuals and on human relationships.

7.1.5 A worldview, a common view at the world in which we live, provides for *mutual understanding*. It allows people to interact, communicate, and coexist. Furthermore, it allows *co-operating*. Co-operation makes more efficient the efforts of individuals to improve their conditions of existence.

7.1.6 Worldview influences individual behavior. A person guided by a worldview of *uncertainty, relativism* and *nihilism* behaves accordingly.

7.2 Dynamics of development of worldview

7.2.1 Tracing the dynamics of the development of the Western worldview, we discover that *it is changing* with the advance of knowledge. In recorded history, it initially was based on *religion*. The world was viewed as an unchanging creation of God. The behavior and relationships of individuals was dictated by the sacred moral commandments given by God. Deviations in views and behavior were considered as sin punishable by God and (by His will) - by the Church. This worldview did not need explanation. It was based on faith. This was a worldview of BEING.

7.2.2 With the increase of knowledge about natural phenomena, the worldview of Being *broadened*. In addition to religion, it was based on *natural philosophy* that applied reasoning for the argumentation of its conclusions and recommendations.

7.3 A worldview based on science – mechanistic worldview

7.3.1 From the middle of the past millennium to the present time, the worldview is being formed by *science*. Science *explains* phenomena by discovering their underlying *processes* and the *mechanisms* responsible for these processes.

7.3.2 I refer the beginning of development of the *scientific* worldview to the middle of the 16th century - time of discovery by Copernicus of Motion as a fundamental notion *independent* from that of Being. Based on this discovery, a mechanistic philosophy was developed by Descartes. It received its substantiation in the theory of classical mechanics by Newton.

7.3.3 Discoveries of Copernicus, Descartes and Newton allowed people to see *our* world from a point of view *different* from that of Being described by religion and natural philosophy. All the natural phenomena were viewed as the manifestations of Motion. This was the **mechanistic** worldview. According to this view, the solar system and the living creatures including Man functioned as machines. Their functioning being subordinated to the laws of mechanics.

7.3.4 Tremendous success of mechanics in the area of technology heightened the prestige of science. Mathematical method, with its preciseness, instilled confidence in the reliability of conclusions based on the mechanistic worldview. The era of Enlightenment had set in. Influence of religious and philosophical ideas of the worldview of Being based on faith and reasoning faded having no experimental substantiation.

It was expected that mechanics would explain all the natural phenomena. The resulting understanding should have helped us to solve our every day problems including those of human relationships.

7.3.5 Gradually, however, observations revealed that the phenomena of life could *not* be explained by mechanics. Newton understood this, saying: "Nature's action are either vegetable…or purely mechanical".

7.4   Evolutionary worldview

7.4.1   A philosophico-scientific discovery, made at the dawn of the 19th century, paved the way for a new view of the natural phenomena related to living creatures. Lamarck discovered a new *fundamental notion* of Origin *independent* from those of Being and Motion and formulated the *process* underlying pertinent phenomena – that of *evolution*. But the grip of the mechanistic worldview was too strong. It is enough to say that Lamarck himself remained influenced by it in his explanation of the mechanisms of evolution. Lamarck's discovery of the process of evolution was not appreciated by his contemporaries.

7.4.2   Fifty years later, Darwin discovered the true mechanisms of evolution (random mutations, heredity and natural selection) and formulated the theory of origin of species. At this time the public was ready to accept a theory which considered and explained phenomena related to living organisms. Furthermore, though the evolutionary theory described *origin of species*, it was viewed (erroneously) as a theory explaining *all* the phenomena of life including *existence of organisms*, first of all - existence of man (and not only his origin). It was another irony of human thought – *too broad* a consideration of a certain theory.

7.4.3   A different general view of the course of natural phenomena has developed based on a newly discovered fundamental notion of Origin and a theory of evolution. We name it the ***evolutionary worldview***. Here again science essentially influenced understanding of the behavior of individuals and of human relationships. They were viewed as a manifestation of a ceaseless struggle in which only the fittest survive. The beliefs, norms, and institutions, which formed the basis of the very existence of mankind, became amenable and furthermore destined to destruction in the course of the all-involving process of flux. The influence of religion and philosophy had already been weakened by the mechanistic worldview and diminished drastically.

7.4.4   Social Darwinism and the Will to Power theory by Nietzsche (which in a modified version served as a philosophical basis for the Nazis' ideology), we name among the extreme social theories based on Darwin's theory. But the first to use Darwin's theory to substantiate his social teaching was Marx.

The following is a concise analysis of Marxist theory.

7.5 <u>Marx's theory of Historical Materialism</u>

7.5.1 The social systems of such thinkers as Rousseau, Hegel, and others who preceded Marx, where *philosophical*, i.e., limited by an introduction of certain notions *describing* the events. Marx was the first who introduced a <u>*scientific*</u> social theory. The theory *explained* the events *by discovering the process and the mechanisms* underlying the events. His particular social theory was based on the fundamental scientific theories of evolution *and* mechanics. A strict formalistic division of mankind into two classes, proletariat and bourgeoisie, reflects the influence of the mechanistic worldview. The evolutionary theory is used by Marx first of all for the justification of an uncompromising class struggle aimed at the annihilation of one class by the other.

7.5.2 A scientific theory *defines the area* of pertinent phenomena under its study. A theory then *explains* the phenomena under study by discovering their underlying process and mechanisms.

Marx defined the area of his studies as that of *class relationships*. He determined their underlying *process* – that of the *struggle for the means of production*. According to Marxist teaching, the struggle for the means of production characterises human relationships throughout the history of mankind. Therefore he named his theory A *Theory of Historical Materialism*. He also defined the pertinent *mechanisms* through which the class struggle is carried out - annihilation of the bourgeois antagonistic class and destruction of its social institutions, expropriation and nationalisation of the means of production, and establishment of the dictatorship of the proletariat.

7.5.3 Neither the evolutionary nor the mechanistic approach to natural phenomena considers *individual* objects. Rather, both general theories deal with the objects characterised by the averaged properties, and with the mass populations. Following this evolutionary-mechanistic view, Marxist theory does not differentiate individuals with their particular circumstances, needs, and aspirations. All are herded into inimical masses of the faceless members of their classes. Everyone can and should be sacrificed for the sake of the class interests. Like a living creature that is not given a chance by the natural selection.

7.5.4 Marx does not limit the substantiation of his revolutionary program by the general scientific considerations. The theory of Historical Materialism also gives an economic argument in the form of a theory of Surplus Value. It says the following.

The value of a product exceeds that of the materials (tools, etc.) plus wages. This *surplus value* is appropriated by the employer. But the surplus value is a result of the *surplus labour* of the worker. Therefore it belongs to the labourers and *not* to the capitalists. Thus the capitalists robbed the workers. Workers are entitled to take back what belongs to them. Since the capitalists will not agree to return what they amassed, the proletarians should annihilate the capitalists, destroy their social institutions, expropriate and nationalise their property, and establish a dictatorship of the proletariat in order to prevent and suppress any dissent or attempts of rebellion.

7.5.5   According to Marxist theory, any means are justified for the achievement of the class aims. "Being determines conscience… Morality, religion…, forms of consciousness…no longer retain semblance of independence. They have no history, no development…" says Marx.

7.5.6   Any belief or view, any institution which does not agree with and does not actively promote the Communist aims, should be destroyed or converted, including family, religion, morals, philosophy, and any spiritual and intellectual opposition. The Marxist understanding of the evolution and mechanics of human relationships did not allow any deviations from the Party line.

7.5.7   The following are the words from the Communist Party hymn.

"We will destroy all and then we will build the New World of ours – Those who were nothing will become everything".

A Communist Party hymn is not just a song – it is a Manifesto, a Program of actions presented in a popular form.

7.6   Refutation of the Marxist theory

7.6.1   *All* the above premises of Historical Materialism are *refuted* by the Theory of Existence.

7.6.2   Based on the Theory of Existence, it is possible to explain why Marx's teaching attracted so many followers and still remains influential in spite of the overwhelming evidence of its insolvency. Marx **promised** his followers the *fulfilment of their needs.* "…Each according to his needs" – this motto attracted masses of the adherents to his doctrine. It is impossible to promise more.

7.6.3   If one asks, "What is everyone busy doing day after day during one's entire life?" —The unifying answer is "Everyone is trying to satisfy the needs necessary for the maintenance of one's existence". This is a simplified formulation of one of the general Laws of Existence, which is valid for every living creature (see *How Man Exists,* 2001).

7.6.4   The theory of Historical Materialism does not consider, and does not explain, all the phenomena embraced by the notion of Existence. As a matter of fact, the area of its consideration is rather limited. Thus, for example, Marxist theory does not explain how *any* natural object, living or inanimate, exists. It does not explain how various individual organisms exist. These phenomena are beyond consideration of the theory of historical materialism. The subject of the consideration of this theory belongs to the area of Existence of man. Yet, even this particular area of natural phenomena is not considered comprehensively by the Marxist theory. It does not describe, and does not explain the processes and the mechanisms of existence of a human organism at the subcellular-cellular, organ-system, and the organism levels. Marx does not suggest theories of physiology and medicine, and other considerations related to health.

7.6.5   Historical Materialism considers human social relationships. It means that this is a theory, which considers phenomena of *existence* within a certain level of organization – the *social* - in relation to a *sole species* – human. It should be classified therefore as a *particular* scientific theory (social theory related to man). Pertinent phenomena belong to the area of Existence therefore Marxist particular theory should have been based on the general Theory of Existence. Marx, however, based his social theory on the theories of evolution and the mechanics. As explained above, a theory, including a fundamental one, can explain *only* the phenomena governed by the process described by this theory. Theories of *evolution* and *mechanics* **cannot** serve as a base for a *social* theory because the social phenomena proceed **not** by the processes of evolution and physical-chemical interactions but by that of adequate functioning discovered by the theory of existence. A *particular* social theory of Historical Materialism, based on the *inappropriate fundamental* theories, inevitably leads to wrong conclusions and recommendations. It is as if one would try to base some particular theory of motion, e.g. the theory of electricity, on the evolutionary theory, instead of the theory of mechanics (see above the Principle of Appropriateness).

7.6.6   Formalistic division of mankind into two hostile classes – proletarians and bourgeoisie, does not reflect the complexity of social relationships.

7.6.7   Marx's conclusion about the necessity and inevitability of annihilation of the social class of proprietors by the proletarians in the course of uncompromising straggle, which he based on Darwin's theory, was erroneous.

This is precisely because of compromise proletarians become the proprietors. The workers *have* "what to lose".

The preceding accentuates the erroneousness of herding individuals into *masses.* Each person is unique. Each has different capabilities, circumstances, and aspirations which should be taken into consideration by a social theory.

7.6.8   It follows from these considerations that the notion of the human relationships *subsumes* that of the class relationships. It follows from the theory of Human Relationships (see further) that *compromise* and *co-operation* – not the ceaseless mortal struggle – form the leading process underlying relationships of people in their effort to improve their conditions. Without compromise and cooperation, the humankind would cease to exist.

7.6.9   A statement that morality and religion (as the bearer of the moral truths) "have no history, no development" does not reflect the reality of prevailing human relationships. Negation of morality is a manifestation of the evolutionary-mechanistic worldview, which guided Marx. The theories of evolution and mechanics do not consider the notion of morality. Morality is irrelevant to the phenomena of the origin of species and of the motion of physical bodies and particles. Morality, however, is an inalienable factor of the existence of man. The theory of existence defines morals as one of the leading mechanisms of human relationships.

7.6.10   The historico-economic substantiation of Marxist teaching does not reflect the reality of human relationships either.

> Engels wrote: "These two great discoveries, the materialistic conception of history and the revelation of the secret of capitalistic production through surplus value, we owe to Marx. With these discoveries socialism became a science." (Socialism: Utopian and Scientific, book against Duhring, 1892).

The means of production, however, is not an absolutely necessary factor for existence. Animals do without the means of production. Humans did without the means of production for the most part of the history of their existence. Thus the main thesis of Historical Materialism of the necessity of the means of production for existence of man is incorrect. What *is* necessary for existence of Man is the <u>society of other men</u>.

A history of mankind is a reflection and a result of the tendency of man to improve one's conditions through active use of extending knowledge on the basis of cooperation (one of the laws of existence of man – see further). Production of the means of production is a manifestation and a particular illustration of development of technology resulting from the use of extending knowledge.

7.6.11 Engels wrote about *surplus value* "that even if the capitalist buys the labor power of his laborer at its full value as a commodity on the market he yet extracts more value from it than he paid for, and that in the ultimate analysis this surplus value forms those sums of value from which are heaped up the constantly increasing masses of capital in the hands of the possessing classes" (Ibid.).

Thus surplus value is presented as a hidden vehicle of capitalistic exploitation and misappropriation of wealth that should have belonged to the workers. But this is precisely what the employee was paid for - to perform work that produces some *value*. A worker gets the wages as payment for the *creation* of the surplus value of a product.

7.6.12 Example: capitalist, who manufactures furniture, invested in the building, equipment, and materials. He pays the workers. A table costs *more* then the wood and other manufacturing-related expenses. This surplus value is a result of workers' labor. But this is precisely what the workers were paid their wages for: for making furniture, whose value is *higher* than the initial expenses. The higher the workers' skill, the higher the surplus value of their labor - the more they are paid. If a worker does not produce a surplus value or demands this surplus value for himself - for what does he expect to be hired and paid the wages? Instead of getting profit, such a manufacturing system is doomed to bankruptcy. We come to a definitive conclusion that by appropriating the surplus value, the capitalist **did not rob** the workers. By paying wages (determined by the market) the capitalist *bough*t the surplus labor, thus the surplus value belongs to the capitalist.

7.6.13 We come to conclusion that Marx's thesis that the workers are entitled to expropriate the other's property is *erroneous*. I name it an **unearned entitlement**.

7.7 Conscience determines being

7.7.1 It follows from the Theory of Existence, that there is certain subordination between the structural-functional levels of existence of man. We name it a *hierarchy* of the levels, according to which the higher level controls the function of the lower ones. The highest level of organization of a man is *social*. It controls the functions of the lower ones, including the organism-behavioral, organ-system, and the subcellular-cellular levels.

7.7.2 Considering the meaning used by Marx, "conscience" refers to the social level. While speaking of "being" or "existence" Marx refers to the lower levels responsible for the physiological functions. When Marx emphasizes the primacy of being over consciousness, he does not consider that at the different levels of organization, existence of man is provided by *different mechanisms* functioning in accordance with certain subordination. This subordination is demonstrated by the ordinary manifestations of human relationships. Practices of everyday life show that the mechanisms providing for the *adequate functioning* at the *social* level (conscience), viz., *reason, morals* and *law* have a primacy over the mechanisms, such as *instincts*, acting at the *lower* levels (being). Most of the individuals in most of the situations are functioning adequately. Individuals control their instincts. This obvious fact demonstrates that <u>conscience</u> determines being in direct opposition to Marx's assertion.

7.7.3   Stalin's regime of fear and Mao's "re-educational" camps were organized following the Marxist thesis that being determines conscience. It was supposed that the Marxist conscience should be hammered in by a suppressing being. In order to give you a moment of relaxation, I suggest an example of a different kind. To prove the leading role of *being,* a historical materialist does not need to put every person in a labor camp. It is enough to lock the door to the toilet, and sooner rater then later the consciousness of any individual will be preoccupied by physiological concerns. This might seem a persuasive example of a being determining conscience. But it is *not*. And my argument against it is that this example is <u>irrelevant.</u> It considers existence at the cellular, organ-system and the organism-behavioral levels, but not at the social level. Physiological needs result from metabolic processes going on at the cellular and organ-system levels. Urges are the manifestations of functioning at the organism-behavioral level regulated by reflexes and instincts. In other words, we do not deal here with the processes and mechanisms of the social level. The only part of this example, which might be referred to the social level, is that an individual is looking for a toilet. This is a direct illustration of reason, morals and law controlling the instinct. In other words, this is an example that conscience determines being, and not the other way around.

7.7.4   I conclude that the assertion that being determines conscience is *erroneous.* This is what differentiates humans from other animals: the human conscience controls the instincts.

7.7.5   Historical materialism is the only *scientific* theory of human relationships which has been widely applied in practice. In spite of its obvious fiasco, it continues to attract followers. It is even more important that Marxist teaching *influences* the social views of a tremendous amount of individuals. Degree of this influence may differ. Some follow it without *consciously* accepting the fact. Others insist that Marx's views are correct in principle, but they were misinterpreted and distorted: "We have not seen a real Marx, yet"- they say.

7.7.6 Our analysis based on the Theory of Existence shows that Historical Materialism is founded on inappropriate fundamental theories, and is presented by erroneous propositions. Those who suggest that we "have not seen a real Marx, yet" – are tragically mistaken. Marxist program was not distorted. On the contrary, it was fulfilled to its miniscule details. And *therefore* it brought much destruction.

7.8 Globalization – a consequence of 200 years of the world industrial development

7.8.1 Still the class struggle, as a way to fulfillment of all needs, keeps its allure. Marxist slogans of the demonstrators against the recent G-8 economic summit in Italy (July 2001) are an example. Economic globalization is considered as an intentional attack plotted today by the big corporations with the aim of the creation of an *Empire* of International Capital.

7.8.2 A particular feature of social phenomena is that the current events often are the results of developments that began much earlier - in many cases – generations ago. It is impossible to understand what happened in Russia in the 20th century without consideration of the events that took place in the 19th century. Therefore an immediate observation and experiment, which proved to be effective methods of study of *motion*, are mostly *inapplicable* for the studies of human relationships. This feature should be taken into account when we try to understand the modern phenomenon of globalization.

7.8.3 The current globalization of market and overall economics is a result of more than *two hundred years* of the world industrial development. Emerged in the 18th century, it was aimed at satisfying of the *basic needs* of the growing population. These needs were food, clothes, means of transportation, and the means of mass production of thereof. During the following two centuries, the *manufacturing capacity* throughout the world in general remained *insufficient* for satisfaction of continuously growing needs. There was a chronic insufficiency of the staple goods. Therefore it was necessary to *expand* the manufacturing base. This resulted in a continuous creation of the new working positions.

7.8.4 As a result of advancement in science, technology, and organization of the process of production countries appeared whose industrial capacities were *sufficient* for satisfaction of the needs of *their* national markets. Local overproduction resulted in temporary economic depressions.

7.8.5   The amount of countries whose national industrial capacity essentially *exceeded* needs of their internal markets grew. In order to keep their growing working force busy, these countries were increasingly selling abroad, thus satisfying the needs of citizens in other countries. This is how the process of modern globalization *started*.

7.9   Global industrial capacity reached a plateau

7.9.1   At the end of the 20th century, the *summary capacity* to produce staple goods necessary to satisfy the basic needs of existence throughout the world reached a level when its further expansion is *not* necessary any more. This does not mean that the needs for the staple goods disappeared. These needs remain. Somewhere there is a need for more clothes and shoes. In another place, more cars are needed. But there is no necessity to build *new* manufacturing capacities to satisfy these needs. Actually, there is a global *over*-capacity. It is regulated by the competition for the markets. Excessive capacities are forced to downsize, or close in the absence of sufficient amount of steady orders.

7.9.2   *Industrial development reached a **plateau** of the summary global manufacturing capacity for production of staple goods necessary for existence.*

7.9.3   A system of international actions (World Trade Organization, G-8 regular summits, at al.), dubbed "globalization", represents an attempt to relief the burden created by the *plateau* (of the global manufacturing capacity).

7.9.4   Every politician in any country speaks of an increase of production and productivity. But the problem is that an increased production of what is already overproduced will not create new jobs, higher wages and economic prosperity, and diminish poverty. The least effective way to deal with the situation, however, is to cling to Marxist slogans of blame and destruction.

7.9.5   It is necessary to manufacture products, for which there is an *unsatisfied* need and *not enough* the existing *manufacturing capacities*. This should stimulate construction of new facilities, opening of new working positions, creation of new, well paid specialties and professions. Consider these historic examples of industrial development when the new manufacturing capacities were necessary in order to satisfy the demands of the consumers. The building of metal ships necessitated construction of new shipyards, increased metallurgic production, and the creation of new professions. These developments resulted in the opening of new highly paid jobs of various kinds. An analogous situation took place with the creation of the car and the airplane manufacturing industries. Development of communication technology, production of computers, and related products is a spectacular most resent example. It led to an astounding growth of prosperity in most countries.

7.10 Basic science – the source of prosperity

7.10.1 All the above examples have a certain common feature. Economic growth resulted from the discoveries of basic science. Yet, the cut of spending for basic science is the preferable way to economize. This refers both to the governments and to the private corporations. Neither governments, nor the companies are willing to take "long-term" and risky projects, though precisely these kind of projects promise the highest return, both economic and social. The French government risked funding the studies by Pasteur. The return was a rehabilitation of the entire industries (manufacturing of silk and of beer and vine, and cattle growing). And above these tremendous economic achievements – development of scientific medicine. Another example – the funding of pioneering research in the area of communication technology by the American government and the private companies. The result again - the economic and social benefits brought by basic research on a global scale.

7.11 A new scientific social theory – Theory of Human Relationships – an alternative to the theory of Historical Materialism

7.11.1 We introduce a *new* scientific social theory. In difference from the theory of historical materialism, the new theory is based *not* on the fundamental theories of mechanics and evolution but on that of *existence*.

7.11.2 The theories of mechanics and evolution study primarily *populations* (e.g., of physical particles or of organisms). Based on these theories, Historical Materialism operates with masses of people. It divides mankind into two inimical classes. And it studies the class struggle for the means of production.

7.11.3 The general theory of existence is centered on the study of *individual natural objects*. Accordingly, the central subject of study of the new social theory is the *human individual.* The *process* that underlies and governs existence of the individuals at the social level of organization is the process of human relationships. Therefore I named the new social theory – a **Theory of Human Relationships.**

7.11.4   The new theory does not claim that it will allow the fulfillment of all the needs of all people. Based on the scientifico-philosophical argumentation, the Theory of Human Relationships suggests that it should help people in their efforts to improve the conditions of their existence. A tendency to improve the conditions of existence is the law of social existence of man discovered by the new theory.

7.12   The new social theory comprises and uses the following laws of nature

7.12.1   *What* is a law of nature is discussed in detail in *How Man Exists* (2001). By our definition, a law of nature is a description of a certain regularity of a fundamental (or a basic) process. Thus we differentiate the laws of physical-chemical interactions, evolution and adequate functioning, or those of *motion*, *origin* and *existence*, correspondingly. Since fundamental processes are acting at all the structural-functional levels of organization, the laws describing their regularities are valid at all the organizational levels. Therefore we name them *fundamental* (general) laws of nature. The law of preservation of energy represents an example of a fundamental law of nature in the area of motion, which is valid for the phenomena of Motion whether at the macro, or the micro levels of organization of the interacting objects.

7.12.2   In addition to the fundamental laws, there exist also the *basic* laws of nature. These laws describe regularities of the basic processes. In difference from a fundamental process which governs phenomena at all the levels of organization, the basic process governs only those phenomena which occur at a certain basic level. Therefore the basic laws are valid for the phenomena taking place at the corresponding basic levels of organization. Though they are narrower, basic laws still embrace very broad areas of phenomena. For example, the laws of classical and quantum mechanics are the basic laws of nature describing phenomena of motion at the macro *or* the micro organizational levels, correspondingly.

7.12.3   The General Theory of Existence discovered the fundamental laws of *adequate functioning* or the *laws of existence*. These are the laws of nature valid for all the natural objects at any organizational levels of their existence, including the social level of existence of man (see *How Man Exists*, 2001).

7.12.4   The First law says that natural objects, including man, have a certain structural-functional organization.

7.12.5 It follows from the Second law that man exists by functioning in accordance to needs directed to the maintenance of his entity.

7.12.6 The Third law explains that human behavior represents a spectrum of *adequate* and *in*adequate functioning. Adequate functioning brings an individual closer to the favorable state at which one exists longer. Whereas the inadequate functioning hinders achievement of the favorable state and thus shortens longevity. (I consider longevity as a quantitative characteristic of existence).

7.12.17 It follows from the 3rd law that the choice of behavior may influence our state and longevity. Acknowledgement of the possibility and of the role of *choice* differentiates the laws of existence from those of classical mechanics. Yet, both kinds of laws reflect *reality*. If you jump up, you inevitably return to the Earth. Laws of *motion* do not assume choice. But if you *choose* to jump from an airplane without a parachute, your *existence* would be shortened as a result of your choice.

7.12.7 The Fourth law says that natural objects including man adjust to conditions of existence.

7.12.8 The Fifth law says that the natural objects exist in-groups. This allows their needs be maximally satisfied. This definitely refers to men. Alone, - an individual perishes. This assertion was valid for the prehistoric man, and remains so for the modern man.

7.12.9 It follows from the Sixth law that in-groups, the adequately functioning individuals *cooperate*.

7.12.10 The 5th and 6th laws contradict the social philosophy based on the evolutionary theory. Thus the evolutionary theory is *inapplicable* for the explanation of the phenomena of *existence*.

7.12.11 These general laws of adequate functioning are applicable for the understanding and explanation of *human relationships* since the pertinent phenomena belong to those of Existence. Therefore they are included and used by the new scientific social theory.

7.13 A law of nature describing human social behavior and relationships

7.13.1 Besides the fundamental and the basic laws of nature, there are also the *particular* laws describing certain phenomena underlain by the *particular processes* proceeding *within* a certain basic structural-functional level. These are *laws* in the sense that they describe persistent regularities and not some accidental coincidences. But we classify most of them as the laws of a certain *specialty* or a field of study. Such as the laws of astronomy, chemistry, or medicine. Here belong, e. g., the laws of infectious diseases discovered by Pasteur and Koch: Infectious diseases are caused by the pathogenic infectious agents (and not by tiredness, exposure to cold, or the crowd condition as such). A certain disease is caused by a corresponding infectious agent – tuberculosis by a Mycobacterium tuberculosis and not by the Vibrio cholerae, which in its turn causes cholera, but not vice versa.

7.13.2 Still, some *particular* laws, which embrace broad areas of phenomena important for man, are classified as the *laws of nature,* for example, the Kepler's laws of motion of planets, laws of electricity, or the laws of behavior of gases.

7.13.3 Proceeding from the above classification, we introduce a law of human social behavior:

Man tends to improve the conditions of one's existence acting in cooperation with the others and employing expanding knowledge.

7.13.4 This law is applicable *within* a certain basic level of existence – social, and for a certain species of organisms – man. Therefore it should be classified as a *particular* law. It embraces a very broad scope of phenomena of an immediate importance for man, therefore we classify it as a *law of nature*.

7.13.5 Thus, the new social theory, which is based on a general theory of existence, uses the general and the particular laws of adequate functioning for the description of social behavior and interactions of people.

7.14 Mechanisms of adequate functioning responsible for the process of human relationships

7.14.1 Historical Materialism names the mechanisms providing for the process of uncompromising struggle for the means of production – annihilation of bourgeoisie, expropriation and nationalization of property, destruction of the long-established basic institutions, and establishment of the proletarian dictatorship.

According to the new social theory, *mechanisms* providing for the process of human relationships of the *adequately functioning people* are **Reason, Morals** and **Law**.

I repeat that these are the mechanisms that provide for the adequate functioning of the people at the social level.

7.15 Consideration of Reason, Morals and Law as the basic mechanisms of the social adequate functioning is <u>not</u> an utopia

7.15.1 The following needs to be considered when the mechanisms of the human relationships are discussed. Differing from the laws of classical mechanics, the laws of existence allow the possibility of *choice*. The laws describe reality. Our existence depends on our behavior to a considerable extent. It presents a *spectrum* of <u>adequate</u> and <u>inadequate</u> functioning (the 3rd law of existence). If adequate functioning *prevails*, individuals achieve their favorable state and therefore exist longer. (Notions of adequate/inadequate functioning are described in details in *How Man Exists*, 2001).

7.15.2 There is nothing utopian in the propositions of the new social theory. It does presume that individuals have different needs, abilities, aspirations, and circumstances, and that they may cooperate or confront each other. The theory of human relationships explains that the adequately functioning individuals tend to improve conditions of existence, which is achieved most efficiently in cooperation and by using expanding knowledge. And that at the social level of organization of man, *adequate functioning* is provided by certain mechanisms. These are *reason, morals* and *law*.

7.15.3 One might argue that the history of mankind and the anthropological findings do not support the thesis of the new social theory that reason, morals and law predominantly govern the human relationships. Each of us knows examples of people acting unreasonably, immorally and lawlessly.

As I said previously, the theory explains that the human relationships represent a *spectrum* of adequate and inadequate functioning. <u>Adequate functioning prevails in nature</u>. This is how nature and man flourish in spite of hardships. When the balance shifts toward the prevalence of *inadequate* functioning, the existence of the entire peoples worsens and shortens. History and anthropology *concentrate* their attention primarily on social disturbances. Much less frequently do they describe the states of cooperation and prosperity, let alone documenting the crucial positive creative role that reason, morals and law have in the existence of the people.

7.15.4 It is possible that the investigators prefer to describe the confrontations hoping that their study might help us to learn useful lessons. It is also a more dramatic and involving reading. I am inclined to explain the obvious bias as follows. Scientists studying human relationships - historians, anthropologists, sociologists, others – are influenced by evolutionary theory. Evolutionary theory considers phenomena related to living creatures. It explains how Man originated. Therefore they use this theory in *their* studies. The problem is, however, that these scientists deal with the phenomena of Existence - **not** of Origin. Guided by an evolutionary thinking, these investigators look for the facts supporting their view, and interpret their findings accordingly. This does not mean that the discovered facts are erroneous. But their interpretation may be biased. Investigators who look primarily for the signs of social calamities come to the conclusion that hostility is the major mechanism of human relationships, and confrontation is the leading way of human interactions. These conclusions are in line with the evolutionary approach to social events. Few, if any, try to explain the social disasters, which they revealed, by the *deviation* from reason, morals and law. And nobody suggests that compromise and cooperation be in fact the *prevailing* ways of social interaction of people. However, if they were not, humankind would cease to exist. This is what the new scientific social theory suggests and explains. No wishful thinking, no utopian fantasies – just plain reality of Existence.

7.15.5   I interpret the anthropological findings concerning the early stages of development of Homo Sapiens as follows. Modern Man exists as a species for about 100 to 120 thousand years. Excavations show that he coexisted with the Neanderthal Man for the first several tenths of thousands of years. A gradual divergence in the social life and development of technologies was observed between these two species. Neanderthal lived in small groups. He used primitive tools, which were not improved essentially. Homo Sapiens united in large groups. They grew even larger during inter-group social gatherings and the trade exchanges. Technology of the tool making increased steadily in its sophistication. Furthermore, the Modern Man manufactured objects of symbolic value, such as beads. He used them for decoration of the dead in increasingly sophisticated burial sites. Findings of the cave art are dated about 40 thousand years back. I suggest that during this seemingly latent period Homo Sapiens developed his basic social mechanisms of adequate functioning. Development of *reason* can be traced not only by the advancement of technology. Equally or even more demonstratively it is reflected in the development of social skills – interaction of large groups of people, trade, sophisticated burials, and the like. The fact that the Modern Men decorated their dead testifies that they developed *religious* beliefs. An increasingly sophisticated social structure characterized by differentiation of labor, differences in the amount of private possessions, etc., demanded an elaborate administrative organization. The latter needed to be maintained by *law*. Thus Homo sapiens developed the social mechanisms of Reason, Morals and Law. As soon as these basic mechanisms of social existence where developed and used, the Neanderthal was ousted. Modern Man proved to be able to populate the Earth. His creative abilities were manifested not only by the biological and technological success, but also by the flourishing of Art. This is how the new sources of knowledge developed.

7.16   Analysis of the social mechanisms of adequate functioning of man

7.16.1   We differentiate individual and collective **reason**. Individual reason allows a person to evaluate a situation and to act adequately. Collective reason develops and promotes broad notions, which influence human relationships. For example, *democracy* and *individual freedom* are the notions produced by a collective reason.

7.16.2   **Morals** – rules of behavior based on experience and beliefs, individual and collective. Religious morals are the broadest in their scope embracing experience and beliefs of many generations of innumerable individuals. Therefore religious morals are viewed as *the* morals to be followed.

Rules of morals are followed at will. They are maintained by public opinion.

7.16.3   Currently an opinion shared by many is that morals (ethics) represent a relative notion – a matter of personal preference, or personal taste. Those who follow this view say "What is immoral for one person might be moral and commendable for the other". My arguments against this philosophy of relativity of morals are based on the scientific Theory of Human Relationships and the Laws of Existence. Those who insist on the relativity of morals proceed from the evolutionary-mechanistic worldview that is currently dominant. The notion of morals is foreign for this worldview because the theories of evolution and mechanics do not deal with the moral problems at all.

7.16.4   In addition to this general cause, there is also a particular one. I differentiate the individual, the group, and the common morals. Individual morals represent the rules of behavior based on experience acquired by an individual through immediate interactions with others and learned from them. Individual morals help a person to exist and survive in the particular social surroundings. Individual upbringing, teaching and experience may differ. Hence the resultant individual morals followed by different persons may differ relative to their circumstances. In other words, *individual* ethics *are* relative. Group ethics embrace collective experience of a group existing under the conditions that are similar for the individual members. A group might be large, consider examples of Victorian, or the Soviet morals, still it is limited. Therefore the *group* ethics are relative too. But the rules of *common* morals follow from experience of humankind. These rules consider all the possible circumstances of uncountable number of individuals. Therefore the notion of *common* morals is **not** relative.

7.16.5 Religious morals represent a reflection of the common morals. The Ten Commandments are not relative. These are the rules of behavior that through generations proved helping all to improve their existence and thus allowing individuals to live longer in a favorable state. Whereas the immoral behavior contradicting the Commandments resulted in suffering of all involved. The victims suffered because of the actions of the perpetrators, while the perpetrators were punished by God.

7.16.6 The problem of morals is so important for existence of man that it is appropriate to expand its discussion in a historic perspective using particular examples. In the times of Plato, a question was posed – "if the Commandments were *given* by God, should we have followed different morals, if He would have given us *different* Commandments?" Countervailing the latter proposition is the notion by the ancients of a Natural Law, according to which, man is genuinely moral. Therefore men would prefer not to harm the others because of the human nature. Cicero, the ancient Roman orator (106-43 BC), spoke of a "true law, right reason, diffused in all men, constant and everlasting". Hence he insisted that it would be impossible to make "robbery, adultery, or the falsification of wills" a positive law, as this would contradict natural law. A question somewhat similar to that, which puzzled the ancients, is known from the time of Einstein: "could God make the world differently?"

7.16.7 We analyze the above based on the scientific Theory of Human Relationships. It follows from the 3rd law of existence that the adequate functioning allows individuals to improve the conditions and thus to achieve a favorable state, and to exist longer. The inadequate functioning, on the contrary, worsens the conditions, hinders the achievement of a favorable state, and shortens longevity. There is no relativity of the adequate or inadequate functioning because these notions concern **all** involved in a social interaction under consideration. We cannot claim that one person's inadequate functioning is other's person adequate functioning. According to the 5th and the 6th laws, adequately functioning individuals exist in groups and cooperate. The 7th law says that those adequately functioning tend to improve conditions through cooperation and the use of knowledge. The laws of nature define adequate functioning as the functioning that promotes the achievement of a favorable state and prolongs existence. Inadequate functioning opposes all of the above and thus shortens longevity. As the other laws of nature, the laws of existence refer equally to each and to all.

7.16.8 I classify behavior that corresponds to common morals as adequate functioning. Thus I exclude the possibility of moral judgment being relative. I qualify as moral the behavior that promotes improvement of conditions and prolongs longevity. I classify the immoral behavior as an inadequate functioning. This is behavior that hinders achievement of a favorable state and thus shortens longevity. Both characterizations concern all the individuals – the actors and those subjected to the action. I assert that moral behavior is preferable for existence not because it might look nice to somebody's opinion or taste. It is preferable because it improves and prolongs existence.

7.16.9 We discovered an amazing correspondence and harmony between religious, philosophical, and scientific understanding of morals. Ten Commandments - a religious statement - describe adequate functioning. Natural law is a philosophical notion. Law of nature is a scientific one. The 3rd law of existence says that the adequate functioning *prevails* in Nature. According to the Theory of Existence, this law is valid for all natural objects – the inanimate and the animate, including Man. Natural Law says that Man is genuinely moral, therefore moral behavior *prevails* in human actions. The harmony is not accidental. All three sources of knowledge – religion, philosophy and science describe Reality of *Our* World. Each source uses its methods of investigation and description but when it concerns *Existence* all come to a harmonious conclusion.

7.16.10 Proceeding from the laws of existence, I answer the questions by Plato and Einstein as follows. God **would not** give Man different Commandments. As a matter of fact (I mean – a scientific fact), He *could not*, because Mankind could not exist following *different* Commandments. I cannot answer whether God could create different physical laws. But if Einstein asked not a *physical*, but a *metaphysical* question – whether God could create a different System of *Our* World as a whole, my answer is **No**. Our philosophico-scientific system of the world is described in the next chapter. It suggests that *Our* World exists as a result of harmonic functioning of the processes and mechanism of interaction, evolution and adequate functioning (pay attention to the notions of Physiology of Nature and of the Principle of Adequate Function, Table1). The process of adequate functioning and its mechanisms, including Morals, are the unalienable components of this general system. We came to conclusion that God could not replace the process of adequate functioning and give men different morals, hence my answer to the question whether He could create *Our* World differently is negative, if the aim of creation was existence of Man.

7.16.11 Ayer – a contemporary philosopher who developed a theory of the relativity and worthlessness of moral ethical judgments, says the following:

> "The fundamental ethical concepts are not analyzable - they are mere pseudo-concepts. The presence of an ethical symbol in a proposition adds nothing to its factual content. Thus if I say to someone, 'You acted wrongly in stealing that money,' I am not stating anything more than if I had simply said 'You stole that money'. In adding that this action is wrong I am not making any further statement about it. It is if I had said 'You stole that money' in a peculiar tone of horror, or written it with an exclamation mark, which adds nothing to the literal meaning of the sentence, but merely expressing 'certain feelings' …In every case in which one commonly would be said to be making an ethical judgment, the function of the ethical word is purely 'emotive' …Moral judgments do not say anything…, they have no objective validity whatsoever…, inasmuch as there is no criterion by which one can test their validity" (Ayer, "Language Truth and Logic", pp. 106-108, 1970).

7.16.12 Our Theory of Human Relationships gives an objective criterion for the moral judgments. The criterion is whether an action or a way of behavior is a manifestation of the *process of adequate functioning*. That is whether it promotes improvement of conditions of existence, brings closer to the favorable state and thus advances longevity of **all** to whom this action, or behavior concerns. These actions and behavior I characterize as being moral, right and good. On the contrary, the actions and behavior that hamper the improvement of conditions, hinder the achievement of favorable state and thus shorten longevity of those involved, I characterize as immoral, wrong and bad. Our criterion is not limited by expression of feelings and opinion, which is legitimate in-itself. We also have an objective, scientifically substantiated standard of judgment based on facts. Nobody can say now that the notion of morals is "relative" and "what is immoral and wrong from a point of view of a one person is moral and right for the other".

7.16.13 **Law** represents the rules of behavior instilled and enforced by an authority.

Our theory differentiates two major kinds of human relationships: relationships between the citizens, and those between the citizens and the Government (State). The theory of human relationships asserts that the Civil Law and the Constitution are *different kinds* of law applicable in *different areas of relationships of citizens*.

Civil Law regulates relationships *between the citizens*. Constitution regulates relationships *between the citizens and the government* (see also *How Man Exists*, 2001).

7.16.14 The fact that the Civil Law, which regulates the relationships of citizens, is issued by the government assures its objectivity. If, however, the government would issue a law that regulates the relationships of the government with the citizens, this would open an opportunity for suppression of the citizens based on the code of law, which is instilled and enforced by the government. To exclude this possibility, a different code of law has been developed – the Constitution. This law is issued *not* by the government, but <u>by the citizens</u> (For practical reasons, Constitution is prepared by the citizen's representatives. It is then debated and approved by the citizens). The differentiation of functions of the Civil Law and the Constitution assures the governing for the people.

7. 17 Constitution <u>should not</u> be opposed to the civil laws

7.17.1 The authors of the US Constitution clearly realized the relation and the difference of functions of these two codes of law. This understanding is reflected in the Constitution in two ways. Firstly, the Constitution proclaims the equality of both codes. It says:

> This Constitution, and the Laws of the United States which shall be made in Pursuance thereof; and all the Treaties made, or which shall be made, under Authority of the United States, shall be the supreme Law of the Land...(US Constitution, Article 6, paragraph 2; 1787).

Thus the Constitution *and* the Civil Law *together* form the Law of the Land. Secondly, the Amendments involving the relationships between the citizens have a special clause concerning this matter. Consider the following examples.

7.17.2   A careful look at the Amendments reveals a certain structural difference between them. Some Articles have a special clause – "Congress shall have power to enforce this article by appropriate legislation", the others do not have this clause. Analysis shows that the Articles, which do not have it, deal with the matters that concern the interactions between the government and the citizens *not* involving the interactions between citizens for the fulfillment of the task. Thus Article 16 speaks of collection of taxes. This is a case of interaction between the government and the citizens. No interaction between the citizens is involved. The additional clause is not needed. And it is absent. The Article 13 abolishes slavery and involuntary servitude. The fulfillment of it involves the relationships between the citizens. But the Constitution does not regulate the relations of citizens between themselves. Therefore the 13th Amendment has a an additional clause that says:

> "Congress shall have power to enforce this article by appropriate legislation".

It means that the Congress will issue some law that will oblige the citizens to observe the abolition in their relationships with one another. The above considerations refer to all Amendments.

7.17.3   This is the point made by our social Theory of Human Relationships based on the thorough comparative analysis of the Constitution and the Civil Law. The theory discovered that neither of these components of the Law of the Land supercedes the other. These are two codes regulating *different* areas of relationships of the citizens. This understanding helps in solving the cases where the Constitution is used in order to oppose and undermine the Law, such as in the attempts to defend antisocial behavior, e.g., spreading of pornography, and the like.

7.17.4   Distributors of pornography, hateful and misogynous "lyrics", hateful speech, and the like, breach the laws. But they insist that their actions are protected by the First Amendment of the US Constitution, which guarantees the freedom of speech. Thus they oppose the Constitution to the Civil Law. I explain that those who oppose the Constitution of the United States to the Civil Law are mistaken. Pay attention to the fact that none of the first 10 Amendments to the US Constitution that form the Bill of Rights has a clause about Congress issuing an additional legislature regulating relationships between the citizens. It is not needed. This is the essence and the meaning of the Bill of Rights that it protects the rights of citizens *in their relationships with the government*. The manifestations of antisocial behavior – TV violence, insulting language, debasement of Art, etc. – all are the cases of relationships of citizens. They are and they should be regulated by the civil law. We will return to this topic when we will discuss the notion of freedom.

7.18 The social *conditions* that are favorable for adequate functioning of people

7.18.1 In *addition* to the process and the mechanisms, the new social theory describes also certain <u>conditions</u> of human relationships, which *promote* and *facilitate adequate functioning*. Among these are **Order, Freedom from Oppression** and *Absence of Unearned Mass Entitlement.*

7.18.2 According to the new theory, <u>Order</u> is a necessary condition that *assures social interactions*. Order is provided by the joint cooperative activities of the citizens and the government.

7.18.3 Another condition that promotes adequate functioning of the citizen is the <u>Freedom from oppression</u> *<u>by an individual, a group, or by the State</u>*.

7.18.4 Freedom does *not* mean the right to do anything that one wishes as is interpreted currently by many. It also is *not* synonymous to "being able to do anything" within the "bounds…determined only by Law" as it is formulated in the French Declaration of the Rights of Man and of the Citizen (1789).

7.18.5 According to the new social theory, Freedom from Oppression means that an individual has the rights to <u>*speak*</u>, to <u>*act*</u>, and to <u>*move*</u> **within the *limits* determined by Reason, Morals and Law.**

7.18.6 It follows from the above definitions that Order does *not contradict* Freedom, and vice versa. On the contrary, Order is necessary for the maintenance of Freedom. Citizens, who are free from oppression, willingly participate in the maintenance of order.

7.18.7 The <u>Absence of Unearned Mass Entitlement</u> is a necessary condition for successful *cooperation* of citizens. Privileges given just for the belonging to a group for some impose an unjustified burden upon others and cause confrontation and disorder. In accordance to the new theory, a privilege can be given only for a certain activity *useful for all*. Entitlement should be *earned*.

7.19 Equality and Justice

7.19.1 Proceeding from these considerations, the new theory presents the following understanding of the notions of Equality and Justice. In accordance with the theory of existence, each individual is unique. Each has different needs, aspirations, capacities, and personal circumstances. Absence of unearned entitlement, i.e., *equality before the law*, in conjunction with the *freedom from oppression* assured by *order*, provide for the *equality of opportunity for everyone*, which is an effective manifestation of *justice for every individual*.

7.19.2 Thus we have a new scientific explanation of how people exist – not through uncompromising fighting of faceless, soulless members of antagonistic groups, but through active *cooperation* of creative individuals whose joined efforts amplify the efficiency of their activities aimed at improvement of their existence.

7.19.3 This new theory is not just a paraphrase of historical materialism. It guides the Human Relationships in a direction that is in opposition to Marxist. This direction is based upon and reflects an entirely new worldview. The new scientific social theory **can** effectively help people in the improvement of their existence, a decisive first step being the change of currently dominant *worldview.*

7.20 The currently dominant worldview should be changed

7.20.1 By our definition, **a *worldview* means – a common general view of the majority at the world in which we live.**

This is the cardinal notion of our Theory of Human Relationships. I suggest that there is no more general, all embracing social notion that would explain the seemingly unexplainable – human behavior and relationships.

The notion deserves a more detailed analysis. Worldview is based on knowledge. The worldview of a modern man is broader than that of a cave man.

Yet it is not a compendium of knowledge. Rather it is an idea, a notion *about* the world in which we live. This vision of the world is *formed by* the current general knowledge and it is shared by the majority. Man always needed some general idea of the world. Without it, man would be lost in the vastness of this world full of unexplainable and unpredictable phenomena. Thus by formulating a new notion of the worldview now, we discovered a common idea, a common understanding by which man was always guided. This is a one of the most general notions of human thought, I suggest.

7.20.2 I characterize the currently dominant Western worldview as **evolutionary-mechanistic.**

7.20.3 The current worldview considers and explains phenomena of *existence* based on the theories of *origin* and *motion*. The guiding *social* ideas following from the <u>evolutionary theory</u> are those of a dominant role of instincts in human relationships, inevitability and necessity of a continuous, uncompromising struggle among peoples, and the constant flux, instability and unreliability of social institutions. Social ideas originated from <u>mechanics</u> are those of uncertainty, relativism and skepticism (for the sake of thereof).

7.20.4 The central problem of our worldview is that the theories of evolution and mechanics do not discover the process and the mechanisms underlying phenomena of existence. Therefore they **cannot** explain our social relationships. Being guided by the social ideas based upon inappropriate scientific foundation, people inevitably come to the erroneous conclusions and act accordingly.

7.21 For the theories of evolution and mechanics, *morals* is an irrelevant notion

7.21.1 The evolutionary–mechanistic worldview is based exclusively on modern science. Religion and (to a considerable extent) philosophy are not considered as the sources of *objective knowledge* – they are dismissed as being *unscientific* (The latter primarily means that they are not based on the results of experiments).

7.21.2 The notion of *morals* is denigrated to the status of a mere matter of personal taste. The theories of evolution and mechanics do not consider the problems of morals - not because these theories are *immoral* – just the notion itself is *irrelevant* to the phenomena of Origin and Motion. There is nothing immoral (moral) in random genetic mutations or in the Brownian motion. In absence of consideration of morals, both theories are *unable* to give any criterion of right and wrong, and in fact dismiss these social notions as being indefinable.

Both theories deal with *populations* (of organisms, or particles). *Individual* does *not* represent an object of their pinpointed consideration. Whereas these are primarily individuals for whose behavior and relationships morals play a crucial role.

7.22 Worldview influences the practice of our social life

7.22.1 The dominant worldview is transformed into the *practice* of our social thinking and acting. It dictates curricular of the teaching programs, directs decisions of the legislators and judges, behavior of the mass media professionals – all those, whose actions influence the conditions of

existence of citizens. It also guides behavior and relationships of all of us
– the *ordinary people*.

The aforementioned refers, first of all, to the *Western* worldview.
However, the authority of modern science is so high everywhere, that the
evolutionary-mechanistic worldview gradually but certainly conquers the
minds of the peoples *throughout the globe*.

7.23 Examples of destructive influence of the currently dominant worldview

7.23.1 It should not present a difficulty to recognize the influence of our
dominant evolutionary-mechanistic worldview in the following examples
of modern beliefs staunchly established in our conscience:

> Dismissing of common morals. Understanding freedom as the
> right to do anything. Biologization of human relationships.
> Acceptance of the primacy of instincts. Disregard and degradation of
> the long-established institutions - family, religion, public opinion,
> and others. Consideration of citizenry not as a cooperative unity, but
> rather a collection of squabbling groups fighting for the unearned
> entitlements. Relativism, intellectual skepticism for the sake of it,
> turning into cynicism.

7.23.2 Manifestations of the social-moral degradation are increasing throughout
the world. All the attempts to thwart the unwanted developments are
ineffective so far. The attempts to explain everything by the poor
conditions are misleading. My explanation is that the current decay is a
manifestation of the influence of the evolutionary-mechanistic
worldview. Sounds too academic, but it is *not*. People are guided by
ideas. This is a specifically human trait. Half a millennium of the
successes of modern science did not pass without a trace. No ideas
proved to be more influential than those of mechanics and evolution. It is
necessary to realize, however, that the theories of mechanics and
evolution obtained a high recognition for their achievements in the
sphere of *technology*, but **not** in the sphere of the *human relationships*.
As soon as we realize the role of our dominant worldview, a lot becomes
to be understood in a new light.

7.24 Notions of a "liberal", "liberal elite", "conservative" - a new understanding

7.24.1 In the light of the above considerations, a new understanding is required for the often used notions of a "liberal", "liberal elite", and a "conservative".

7.25 Modern liberals

7.25.1 Modern liberals, or the "left" (a revolutionary connotation) are those who are being guided by the currently dominant evolutionary-mechanistic worldview, independently of whether or not they realize it (most do not). They wish everybody to be satisfied and well. But misguided by their worldview they accept unbridled freedom, primacy of instincts, subdivision of the nation into endless amount of quarreling groups, relativism, nonjudgementalism, etc., as the necessary *manifestations of progress*. This is where "progress" guided by the evolutionary-mechanistic worldview leads them. Recent example: a 14-year-old killed his teacher by a gunshot into the face from point blank range. On television, the crying unfortunate wife of the slain said that she *could not judge* behavior of the murderer because she was *uncertain* whether her judgement would be "objective" (typical nonjudgementalist assertion) - an obvious demonstration of the enormous power of the worldview, if even the wife of a killed teacher cannot characterize the murder as an immoral, criminal and unacceptable act.

7.25.2 In different degree, many cling to the Marxist ideology (e.g., put the blame on others, fight for the (unearned) group entitlements). The reason is the same – a current dominant worldview.

Few of these would be well wishers approve the unwanted developments, such as destruction of family, illegitimacy, or the degrading influence of pop-culture. But most consider them as the *inevitable* by-products of progress. Hence their conclusion: *nothing can be done*. Moreover, *nothing should be done* since it may curtail our freedom.

7.26 Liberal elite – who are they?

7.26.1 Who are this enigmatic "liberal elite", so often talked about by the conservatives, but never pinpointed? Understanding of the role of a worldview in human relationships allows us to name them without giving offence. This is *not* the aim of this study to insult. Our aim is to *understand* and *explain* human relationships *based on a theory of existence*.

7.25.2 The liberal elite are those educated and particularly knowledgeable about the basics of modern science and modern philosophy, who turned the dominant worldview into their personal belief. The fact of development of liberal elite among those educated and the brightest, and their according actions reflects in itself a tremendous influence of the worldview on behavior of individuals. They actively and forcibly apply their views in the practice of human relationships.

7.26.3 Those belonging to the liberal elite fulfill their official duties proceeding from their beliefs and instill their progressive, scientifically substantiated views into the minds of others. The young represent their most receptive audience, being free of personal life experience and eager to perceive the modern and progressive. Intelligently advanced, those belonging to the liberal elite, usually occupy respected social positions, which allow them to influence the *minds* and the *fates* of many citizens. Here belong many of the teachers of schools and universities, governmental administrators, politicians, journalists, authors and performers, and many others. They are the bearers, disseminators, and active implementers of the current evolutionary-mechanistic worldview.

7.27 A worldview is a result of development of common knowledge

7.27.1 The clarification of the notions of the modern liberals and of the liberal elite is *not an attempt to put the blame for the problems of society on some citizens.* I do not look for the "guilty". Rather I explain what is going on. <u>A worldview is a result of the development of knowledge</u> - **not** a result of activity of a certain group of people. A majority of people participates in the development of a common worldview by introducing new ideas, making discoveries, implementing them, and by teaching, disseminating, and using the increasing knowledge.

7.27.2 The experimental method proved itself to be a more effective way of acquisition of knowledge than the passive observation practiced by natural philosophers. Motion happened to be an area of natural phenomena most amenable for its study by the experimental method. Moreover, phenomena of motion – mass, speed, acceleration and others, are measurable and calculable. By using mathematics, experimental method acquired preciseness. Based on the knowledge obtained through the ages of gradual development of the experimental method, Copernicus

(1473-1543) came to the discovery of Motion as a fundamental notion *independent* from that of Being. (Aristotle considered motion as one of the manifestations of Being).

7.27.3 Thanks to advancement of experimental method and mathematics, Motion replaced Being as the central subject of studies for millennia. Francis Bacon (1561-1626), by introducing induction, organized the way, by which knowledge was acquired. Based on these ideas, tremendous discoveries in the area of Motion were made (Galileo, 1564-1642; Kepler, 1571-1630; and others). Descartes (1591-1661) developed mechanistic philosophy. Newton (1642-1727) discovered the fundamental process of motion - physical interaction, and its mechanism – gravitation. The study of Motion thus became a modern science - a human investigative activity aimed not only at discovery of phenomena, but also of their underlying processes and mechanisms. Knowledge of the latter allowed explaining *how* the phenomena occur. An explosion of technological discoveries followed immediately.

7.27.4 It was logical and inevitable that the social philosophers, such as Comte (1798-1857), one of the founders of social sciences, considered the *scientific* view at human relationships as most "positive" and "progressive". The science upon which Comte based his social theory was mechanics. Marx developed further the idea of basing social views on science by employing the evolutionary theory.

7.27.5 Our contemporaries advanced and disseminated the evolutionary-mechanistic social worldview with a particular verve. It is enough to name B. Russell (1872-1970) with his denunciation of religion, and with the essentially useless application of mathematical logic and expressions in social discourse. Or Ayer (1910-1989), who claimed morals to be just an "emotive" expression of opinion that cannot be substantiated because of the *absence* of a "criterion for determining of validity of ethical judgement". The today nonjudgementalism finds its validation in the claims similar to those by Ayer that morals are merely expressions of somebody's subjective opinion.

7.27.6 Example of a straightforward use of a mechanistic approach to analysis of social phenomena is represented by the *Theory of Justice* by J. Rawls (1971). This author suggests a hypothetical way to achieve justice as fairness. He deprives individuals of knowledge about their race, sex, religion, economic and social status, capacities, and ideological inclinations. According to the theory, under this veil of ignorance the individuals become *equal* and act in the common interests because they do not know their own. I suggest that the theory of justice uses for the study of social relationships a method of *simplification* successfully used in physico-mathematical studies. For example, when we study the dynamics of gases we simplify the conditions by assuming that all the gas particles are *equal* by their size and mass. This simplification does not considerably distort reality and allows us to find out important regularities. If Rawls would study physical aspects related to human individuals, e.g., the time of a fall of several divers in a pool, he could disregard all of the above social categories without any distortion of reality. But rendering unique individuals into "equal" physical units devoid of any social characteristics excludes the possibility of any meaningful explanation of their social relationships. We do not need to deprive people of their human features to explain mutual cooperation. Our theory of human relationships explains that the adequately functioning individuals tend to exist in-groups and collaborate, which behavior is most conducive for the improvement of conditions of their existence (the 5th, 6th, and 7th laws of existence).

7.27.7   The theory of *Sociobiology* is introduced by E.O. Wilson (1975). It explains social behavior of man based on the evolutionary theory. Immediately, Wilson comes in to contradiction with the reality of human relationships. He acknowledges that his theory cannot explain human collaboration and mutual help, manifestations of which he characterizes as *altruism*. Explanation that altruism reflects only the relationships among relatives who are motivated by the maintenance and spread of their genetic pool is not corresponding with reality. This is the fundamental problem of a theory, which is trying to explain human *existence* proceeding from a theory of *origin* of species. A central object of a social theory should be the interacting individuals and **not** the populations, such as the species or the masses. Man exists as a result of the prevalence of adequate functioning at all the levels of organization including the social one. As our social theory explains, Reason and Morals are the basic mechanisms of the relationships of adequately functioning individuals. This is how the problem of *altruism* is solved. Journalists name E.O. Wilson as a modern Darwin. This is an example of a journalistic logic. We know Darwin (though not modern) as an *author* of a theory of origin of species. Why name *Darwin* a scientist who *applied* the theory of origin of man for the explanation of existence of man?

7.27.8   These views find a broad acknowledgement in the West. The social theories of Bertrand Russell and John Rawls represent an essential component of the university curricula. A. J. Ayer was knighted by the British crown. His book was translated in several languages. It is appropriate to emphasize that its first edition appeared in 1936, the time when Hitler and Stalin established their State power and where accumulating their forces for the worldwide expansion. Western enthusiastic support of the philosophical works, which negated role of morality, reflects the ideological atmosphere created by the evolutionary-mechanistic worldview, which consequentially lad to the immoral nonjudgementalistic Munich agreement and its consequences.

7.28 Modern liberalism is not a result of a left-wing conspiracy

7.28.1 Our brief review considers the known historical facts from a different angle. Its aim is to demonstrate that the current dismal state of social behavior and relationships of the majority is not a result of some "left-wing conspiracy", as many conservatives are inclined to suggest. Rather most of the manifestations of social decay are the result of a long-lasting process of development of an evolutionary-mechanistic worldview and its dominant guiding influence.

7.29 An equivocal role of Enlightenment

7.29.1 Sometimes we hear complaints that the Enlightenment, though it brought us progress, deprived us of the ability of moral judgements. These utterances are usually voiced in a subtle way – nobody dares to "blame science" for our faulty behavior. (Isaia Berlin is the most vocal critic of Enlightenment. His criticism, however, is somewhat different. It is directed against *philosophy* of science. While I concentrate attention on the *science* itself). These complaints *do* have certain merits. The enlightenment initiated the era of a guiding influence of science on general human thoughts. Fundamental scientific theories – those of mechanics, then evolution and now of evolution *and* mechanics, formed the basis of our currently dominant worldview, including the view at social relationships. These theories explain Origin and Motion. They *cannot* explain the phenomena of Existence, to which the human relationships belong. In particular, these scientific theories do not consider the role of morals – a key notion of human relationships. Instead of blaming science, we should blame ourselves for the misuse of the fundamental scientific theories for the explanation of natural phenomena, which these theories are not supposed to explain.

7.30 Conservatives are even in a worse position then liberals are – they do not have a theory to rely upon

7.30.1 Conservatives, - i.e., those who *oppose* the dominant social worldview - are even in a worse position than the liberals are. Conservatives do not have a scientific theory to base their dissenting views upon. Some try to appeal to religious teaching, others to reasoning illustrated by the facts of life, which show a deepening cultural decline. But religion does not have its former widespread authority – precisely because of the dominance of the evolutionary – mechanistic worldview. And the facts of decay are viewed as being the *inevitable* consequences of progress based on the dominant worldview.

7.30.2 It should be emphasized that the current worldview remains *dominant* for the conservatives as well. This is illustrated by the examples of immoral laws issued by the conservative politicians.

7.30.3 Not having a scientific theory explaining phenomena of Existence, including the *social existence* of Man, deprives both the liberal and the conservative citizens of a scientifically substantiated guidance toward improvement of their social conditions. It also prevents them from using a vast social knowledge provided by other general sources, in particular by religion and philosophy.

7.31 Argument for anti-Americanism

7.31.1 The evolutionary-mechanistic worldview is a product of development of Western culture. Taking into consideration its degrading influence on human relationships, it is no wonder that it provokes resentment throughout the world. It is especially manifested by anti-Americanism.

7.31.2 It is an objective reality that American pop-culture is a bearer of ideas of immorality, blasphemy, violence, and the like. Spread throughout the world by the movies, TV, videos, and recordings, these ideas corrupt the youth.

7.31.3 Destructive influence of modern popular culture is not limited by the sphere of art. It shatters the very foundations of the human social relationships. Notions of love, decency, mutual trust, mutual respect, individual responsibility, and honor – all are vanishing not being supported by the cultural considerations. Pop-culture distorts the human relationships. It should be opposed rather then emulated.

7.31.4 The easiness of penetration by the American pop-culture of the other national cultures can be explained as follows. Modern American culture is associated by many with the American economic success. But the economic success is a result of the freedom from oppression protected by the US Constitution and persistently maintained by the citizens. (In our further discussion, I will return to the topic of role of freedom).

7.31.5 The degrading character of the modern culture whether it is American, Western, or international is an inevitable consequence of the evolutionary-mechanistic worldview devoid of the leading mechanisms of human social relationships – Reason and Morals.

7.32 Marxist and Radical-fundamentalist anti-American ideologies *merge* being based on a common evolutionary-mechanistic worldview.

7.32.1 Two ideologies claim to be the defenders of the poor and protectors of the entire world against degrading influence of pop-culture. These are *Marxism* and *religious radical fundamentalism*. Seemingly disparate, these ideologies in fact have a lot in common because both are based on the evolutionary-mechanistic worldview.

Modern Marxists declare the slogans of struggle between the world proletariat and the imperialist West. The poverty of developing countries they explain by the imperialistic policies of the industrialized countries, first of all, the US. Their way to solution of the problem of destitution is to oppose any efforts of international cooperation and demand of a sort of "global 'welfare' program" for all the oppressive and kleptomaniac political regimes. Influence of the evolutionary-mechanistic worldview on the modern Marxists and all their sympathizers is obvious. Division into antagonistic classes. Blaming of the others. Call to uncompromising straggle with anyone who opposes their views. Demand of unearned mass entitlement in the form of restitution.

7.32.2 Religious radical fundamentalism combines the commonplace Marxist rhetoric with the accusations of a cultural-social character. Here belong the charges of a degrading effect of modern culture and of destructive influence of the excess of freedom. These accusations are supposed to justify the claims of internal political control and imposition of dictatorship over their compatriots, and execution of a program of muss destruction throughout the world having as its ultimate goal an installation of their ways throughout the world. This again is a Marxist-kind objective.

7.33 Refutation of the premises of the Marxist and radical-fundamentalist ideologies

7.33.1 The major common global aspect of *both* ideologies is the premise that an economic success of a nation is necessarily a result of robbery of the other peoples. Blind aggressive anti-Americanism practiced by certain governments and non-governmental organizations, and by the bloody radical movements, is charged primarily with the claims that Americans are exploiting other peoples, achieving success at somebody's expense. This is a typical Marxist proposition.

7.33.2 The Marxist view of human relationships is currently the <u>sole</u> view that is based on a *scientific social theory* – that of Historical Materialism.
The theory of Human Relationships described briefly in this *Tractatus* presents an <u>*alternative* scientifically substantiated</u> approach.

7.33.3 It is necessary to understand the roots of success of the efforts of Americans to improve their economic conditions. *Americans are more successful then others because they are the freest people in the world.* An individual free from oppression can overcome enormous difficulties and achieve the maximum possible. Freedom from oppression - this is what deserves to be emulated.

7.33.4 Dictatorship, submission, and exploitation of ones own nation and others do not bring an economic success. They also do not bring the improvement of conditions of existence of those subdued. Consider the Soviet Empire. It was the most vast country in the world, abounding with natural recourses, and comprising different colonized nations and the satellites. All the peoples, including the Russians, were kept under hard and fast rules of a unified dictatorship of those who claimed that they knew the ultimate truth about human relationships. In less than a century, all the natural resources were squandered and wasted. It is necessary to have in mind that this was the abundance of natural recourses that allowed the USSR to exist as long a time as it did. Another source of its sustenance was the cruelest regime of exploitation of its citizens in the labor camps and beyond. The cause of a progressive impoverishment of the Soviet people was the *absence of freedom from oppression* because oppression thwarts the creative potential of people. Without a creative initiative of the free people, an economic success is unachievable.

7.34   Finland – freedom from oppression

7.34.1   For the doubters, I have another example – Finland. Initially, this country was a part of the Soviet Union. A tiny strip of the Northern periphery of a huge empire, it would become a place of exile for the hundreds of thousands. It happened, however, that Lenin allowed Finland to secede in order to demonstrate that the Soviet republics could exercise a choice of belonging to the USSR at the time of its formation. In contrast from the USSR, Finland does not enjoy the abundance of natural recourses. Harsh climate, rocks and tundra – these are its primary environmental features. Yet, instead of becoming a large labor camp populated by poor people dying of chronic starvation, Finland turned into a prosperous country. Nobody could claim that the Finns robbed someone, whether inside or outside of their country. Their success does not have an explanation from Marxist point of view. The new social theory explains the success of Finland primarily by the fact that its citizens are free from oppression. This is the creative diligent effort of the free people who tend to improve the conditions of their existence through collaboration and use of extending knowledge. This applies to any nation that chooses freedom from oppression as a basis of its politico-social system independently of its prevalent religion.

7.35   There cannot be "too much" freedom from oppression

7.35.1   Critics claim that there is "too much freedom" in the Western countries, especially in the US. In the light of the above analysis, it is necessary to define what is meant by the notion of *freedom*. There cannot be too much of the *freedom from oppression*. That is *the freedom to speak, to do and to move exercised within the limits of reason, morals and law*. Instead of being an impediment, freedom from oppression is a necessary condition for the economic success.

7.35.2   The United States represent a unique example. America accepted scores of individuals from all the countries of the world and gave them the freedom to speak, to do and to move so that they could exercise their creative capacities at maximum and thus improve their existence. The newcomers eagerly amalgamated with the rest of the population. They actively accepted and absorbed the views expressed in the US Constitution. Nobody forced them. This is how the American Nation is being maintained. Individuals draw strength from the roots of the nation and contribute into the common success by doing their day-to-day work as efficiently as only the *free people* caring of their existence may do.

7.36 Social-cultural problems of America and the West are caused primarily by the dominance of the evolutionary-mechanistic worldview

7.36.1 We start with some examples of a social-cultural degradation taking place in the US.

In the US and other Western countries freedom is understood as the right to do anything not forbidden by law (best scenario), or just to do anything (worst scenario). *Reason and morals are not followed - primarily as a consequence of influence of the modern worldview.* Neither reason, nor morals are considered by the theories of evolution and mechanics. Only the Law remains.

7.36.2 However, all three basic mechanisms of the social existence of man should be appropriately used in the relationships of citizens. Reason and morals regulate adequate functioning of individuals. Since most of the citizens in most of the situations behave adequately, reason and morals proved to be the *leading* mechanisms of human relationships. Law has its important role, but alone it is incapable to regulate the nuances and complexities of human relationships.

7.37 Law should be based on Reason and Morals

7.37.1 The major function of law is to prevent the citizens from harming each other physically, financially or morally. To fulfill this function most efficiently, *law itself should be based upon reason and morals.* This principle is neglected by the Western judicial system.

7.37.2 In the US, the interests of a criminal are protected at the expense of the society of diligent citizens. This is immoral and unreasonable. For example, it is a law that a criminal should not cooperate with the authorities protecting the citizens. The law advises that anything that the suspect says could be used against him, so it is in his interests to say nothing. His silence is protected by law, instead of serving as indirect evidence of a possibility of unlawful actions on the part of a suspect who refuses to cooperate.

7.37.3 Immoral and unreasonable laws undermine the authority of the State and cause serious harm to its citizens. Another example of such an American law is the one that allows the citizens to receive money for litigation. This law demoralizes. It distorts normal human relationships. Citizens hunt one another hoping to get unearned money. The most frequent

75

targets are doctors and employers. As a result, the patient-doctor and the employee-employer relationships, which play crucial role in our every day life, are perverted.

7.37.4 American justice is based on a principle that a person is presumed innocent until proven guilty. Physicians are the only category of individuals presumed *guilty* from the moment the complaint is filed. Furthermore, it is almost impossible for a doctor to prove one's innocence because nobody is concerned about justice – it all is a matter of money (unearned and undeserved money, mind you).

7.37.5 Businesses, which employ thousands of people, and manufacture hundreds of useful products, go bankrupt or pay exorbitant ransoms to the lawyers and complainers. First of all - the lawyers.

7.37.6 Lawyers select all the jurors. This negates the idea of the institute of an objective jury.

7.38 Misinterpretation of the Bill of Rights

7.38.1 Freedom of speech as it is practiced in the US is a demonstrative reflection of the interpretation of the notion of freedom as a right to do anything. Any expression, no matter how offensive, insulting, or dirty, is considered to be acceptable, and moreover – protected by law. Unfortunately this practice is emulated throughout the world with a disastrous effect.

7.38.2 Americans refer to the 1st Amendment of the Constitution that prevents Congress from "abridging the freedom of speech, or of the press". It is a bitter irony that in the US, authors and performers of dirty "lyrics" and TV shows, propagators of the blasphemous, hateful and racist materials, and pornographers masquerade themselves as the staunch adherents of the Constitution. They insist that their antisocial activities are protected by the 1st Amendment.

7.38.3 Our Theory of Human Relationships classifies social relationships of citizens into two categories: relationships *between the citizens and the State*, and those *between the citizens themselves*. Relationships between the citizens and the State are regulated by the Constitution. Whereas those between citizens are regulated by the Civil Law.

7.38.4 Theory explains (see *How Man Exists*, 2001) that The 1st Amendment of the Constitution protects the freedom of speech of the citizens *in their interaction with the government (State)*. First Amendment does *not consider* and therefore does **not regulate** (protect or otherwise) the speech that refers to *interactions among citizens*. As a matter of fact, the whole Bill of Rights comprising the first ten Amendments is a document which affirms and protects certain rights of the citizens <u>in their interactions with the State</u>. But *none* of these Amendments, including the 1st, regulate the relationships of citizens with one another.

7.38.5 Hateful, blasphemed, racist and otherwise insulting expressions and bad language are the manifestations of relationships of citizens *with each other*. They should be regulated by the Civil Law based on consideration of *reason* and *morals*.

7.38.6 Misinterpretation of the notion of freedom, immoral laws, and other manifestations of inadequate social functioning are characteristic not only for the United States. These are the consequences of the currently dominant worldview. A decisive way to oppose them is not to cling to the Marxist or fundamentalist ideologies – themselves based on the evolutionary-mechanistic worldview – but <u>to change the worldview</u>.

7.39 Dominance of the evolutionary-mechanistic worldview is the leading cause of the world social-cultural degradation

7.39.1 Western and particularly American social-cultural relationships of the citizens need a decisive reconsideration and change because they thwart the efforts of improvement of the conditions of existence. In order for the change be effective, it is necessary, first of all, to understand what drives our society and the entire world toward self-destruction. **Our analysis of the facts of our everyday life leads us to conclusion that the cause of the socio-cultural degradation is the evolutionary-mechanistic worldview**.

7.39.2 One might be confused by my statement that some scientific theories of biology and physics, which seem so remote from our every day relationships, play such a crucial role in our social and cultural life. Furthermore, one may say that most of the ordinary people who are not working in the areas of biology or physics, do not even know the theories of evolution and mechanics. Definitely, they do not know these theories in details. This is true.

7.39.3 But our worldview, though based upon knowledge, is *not a compendium* of knowledge. Few people are immediately involved in the studies of geophysics, astronomy and similar disciplines. But the majority knows that the Earth is not flat. That it does not rest upon the backs of elephants, or turtles. It is common knowledge that the Earth represents a globe moving in the space. Many even know that it moves around the sun, and not vise versa.

7.39.4 *I introduced the notion of a worldview in order to explain how our collective idea of the world in which we exist influences our behavior and relationships in general.*

7.39.5 Still, a staunch opponent might say that there are *masses* of poor and illiterate who are unaware of any achievements of modern human knowledge, therefore they are not influenced by the evolutionary-mechanistic worldview, yet they do listen to and follow the calls of Marxists and radical fundamentalists. This argument, however, I consider as *supporting* my statement of the guiding role of the evolutionary-mechanistic worldview rather then refuting it. Though these militant calls are based on an erroneous philosophical platform, they attract followers because they give **some** explanation to the terrible plight of the poor. They say what to do about it, and what awaits their followers in case of success. Modern Marxists explain the poverty by the imperialist policies of some governments - first of all of the US, and also of the international Corporations. Radical fundamentalists use the same tactics of blaming the others. Furthermore, their targets are the same – America and the imperialists. Considering their particular audience, fundamentalists exploit some religious notions, such as Great Satan, infidels, and the like, but this does not change the essence of their ideas that somebody – not them – is responsible for the plight. The way to solution is analogous: to destroy and to expropriate. Some difference is in emphases: modern Marxists preach redistribution and expropriation. Fundamentalists call to destruction. Those who follow these calls are promised fulfillment of their needs – on Earth, or beyond. The fact itself that these calls are followed serves as an obvious confirmation of the guiding role of the currently dominant evolutionary-mechanistic worldview.

7.40 My answer to the propaganda of the blame and destruction

7.40.1 My answer to the above propaganda of blame and destruction follows from the new theory of human relationships, which refutes and replaces Historical Materialism. A general feature characteristic for all the nations where poverty prevails is that their citizens are governed by oppressive regimes. There is nobody to blame for the plight of the poor but their oppressive leadership. Freedom of an individual from oppression by a state, or by a group, or by the other individuals is the key to resolution of the problem.

7.41 The American poor

7.41.1 What about the poor Americans? Instead of sloganeering, we should carefully consider *who* are these individuals. These, first of all are the recent immigrants from poor countries, where they were oppressed and remained uneducated and indigent. The US is not supposed to take these individuals on a permanent support just because they are poor. It depends primarily on these individuals how actively and efficiently they choose to use their freedom from oppression. Long term practice shows that the immigrants and their descendants do extremely well becoming Americans, which demonstrates that individuals do posses a great constructive-creative capacities. What are needed for them to improve their conditions are the individual freedom and the willingness to use this freedom by way of adequate functioning.

7.42 The poor among Black Americans

7.42.1 To be honest and consistent in our study, we should consider the situation of the Black Americans. American blacks are, of course, not a homogenous group. Every person is unique. Their conditions vary. Not all of them are poor. Most are not. Still there are many experiencing deprivation. My explanation to these facts may sound unexpected. I suggest that those who are behind are **not free from oppression**. Definitely, they are not oppressed by the American government. They also are not oppressed by individuals. They are oppressed by a *group*. This group is the *modern black leaders*. This is an elite group of politicians guided by the Marxist-fundamentalist ideology. Being staunch believers and practitioners of a radical version of the evolutionary-mechanistic worldview, they impose their ideas of blaming the others – imperialists, whites, the successful blacks – everybody, but themselves. This political elite should instruct and lead their constituency toward the use of freedom for the active betterment of their conditions through self-reliance and collaboration with the rest of the citizenry. Instead - they call for confrontation, hatred of whites, and self-isolation. They demand unearned entitlements in the form of various privileges, reparations, etc. This self-serving propaganda is supported by many well to do Americans – white and black, themselves guided by the evolutionary-mechanistic worldview, though in a less radical form. Solution of the problem is in the change of the worldview.

7.42.2 *African American* is a divisive term. By the origin of our ancestors, all of us are African Americans, because all men originated from Africa. By belonging to one Nation, all of us are *Americans* independently of the color of the skin. A Nation is not a gathering of scattered inimical groups and aloof individuals. Proceeding from the laws of existence, the Theory of Human Relationships explains that *Nation is a unity of self-relying citizens immediately (directly) interdependent in the maintenance of their entity.* The tighter is the union among the individual citizens, the more each of them may achieve in improvement of conditions of their personal existence and of the Nation as a whole. This unity and the resulted collective achievements form the basis of Patriotism.

7.43 The currently dominant evolutionary-mechanistic worldview is the primary cause of the worldwide socio-cultural degradation. This worldview should be replaced.

7.43.1 Thus we came to the conclusion of our study of the influence of science on human relationships. We introduced the notion of a *worldview* – that is a common idea, common understanding of the world, in which we live. And we revealed its role in social behavior and interactions. Then we showed that the modern worldview is based on the knowledge provided by science. This allowed us to explain *how the influence of science on the human relationships takes place.*

7.43.2 The study shows that our worldview is based on the scientific theories of evolution and mechanics. We introduce an idea that the **evolutionary-mechanistic worldview** is *unable* to guide human social relationships so that to help the humankind to improve the conditions of existence.

7.43.3 First of all, our dominant worldview is narrow-minded in a *scientific* sense. The theories of mechanics and evolution explain *only* the phenomena of Origin and Motion. These theories are *unable* to explain phenomena of *Existence* – the area of natural phenomena, to which social relationships belong.

7.43.4 This means that our worldview is incomplete in its *scientific understanding* of Nature – it does not include phenomena of Existence.

7.43.5 Furthermore, our current worldview is scientifically incompetent. Precisely because they cannot explain Existence, the theories of evolution and mechanics *cannot be applied* for the guidance of social relationships.

7.43.6 Being based on an *inappropriate scientific foundation*, our dominant worldview is misleading as it concerns the human relationships.

7.43.7 This is not all. There is still another aspect in which the *narrow-mindedness* of our worldview is manifested. It becomes clear from our definition of the notion of worldview that it should be based on *all* current knowledge. The presently dominant worldview, however, employs the knowledge from <u>only a</u> <u>one source</u> - namely *science*, while other general sources are *neglected*. This in particular refers to *religion* and *philosophy* – the sources, which through millennia accumulated vast knowledge in the area of human relationships.

7.43.8 Thus, we have undertaken a scientifico-philosophical analysis of the current state of the human relationships. We came to a substantiated conclusion that our relationships are based on an unacceptably narrow and, furthermore, inappropriate base.

7.43.9 *This disclosure allows us to reveal a major common cause of many of our burning every day social problems: this is our evolutionary-mechanistic interpretation of human behavior and relationships.*

7.43.10 We realize that such a complex, versatile area of existence of man as the social problems cannot be explained by a sole cause. For example, *overpopulation* is a cause of very serious social problems not immediately related to our worldview But the presence of other causes does not diminish the degrading role played by our inappropriate worldview. (On the problem of overpopulation, see further - Religion).

7.43.11 Knowing the major cause of our socio-cultural problems, we may look for the ways to its elimination. The most effective one is to develop and use a <u>different worldview.</u>

7.44   A new worldview

7.44.1 As we now realize, people have always had a common idea about the world. This idea did not remain immutable. It changed with the development of knowledge. For the purpose of clarity, I should again analyze briefly the stages of development of worldview. In modern time, the worldview is based on science. In the 17th and 18th centuries, the Western worldview was based on the new knowledge summarized by the philosophy of Descartes and the scientific theory of Newton. This was a **mechanistic** worldview. People saw all the natural phenomena as the manifestations of mechanical motion. The solar system and the Man were viewed as machines.

7.44.2 In the 19th century, the idea of evolution developed by Lamarck and scientifically substantiated by Darwin conquered the minds. The worldview transformed. All the phenomena were viewed as the manifestations of the evolutionary changes. This was the **evolutionary** worldview.

7.44.3 In the 20th century, influenced by the discoveries of quantum physics initiated by the theories of Planck and Einstein, the worldview transformed further. Currently, the Western worldview is **evolutionary-mechanistic**. Many factors resulted in a *worldwide spread* of this modern worldview. Among the factors, which promote the evolutionary-mechanistic worldview, the main factor is the authority of science.

7.44.4 The essential role in the dissemination and assurance of a global influence of the current worldview was played by contemporary communication technology. In our time, ideas and images reach the global audience with the speeds of sound and light. Proceeding from the evolutionary-mechanistic worldview, individual behavior and the human social relationships are guided by the ideas of uncertainty, relativity, mutual animosity, amorality, and immorality. The attempts to resist and countervail the degrading socio-cultural influence of the dominant worldview proved to be counterproductive because the opposition itself is influenced by the evolutionary- mechanistic view on the human relationships.

7.44.5 It is necessary to realize that the evolutionary-mechanistic view at the world increasingly dominates the common worldview because there is no other scientific theory able to describe Nature from a point of view different from those of evolution and mechanics.

7.44.6 We introduced a scientific theory, which describes and explains phenomena of Existence (see *How Man Exists*, 2001). Our theory does **not** contradict or negate the theories of evolution and mechanics. The new theory considers a sphere of natural phenomena different from those of Origin and Motion. Human relationships belong to this sphere – the sphere of *existence*.

7.45   A Worldview of Existence

7.45.1 Having a scientific theory and the laws of existence, we can see Nature from a point of view different from those of evolution and mechanics. **Now we can develop a New Worldview – the WORLDVIEW OF EXISTENCE.**

7.45.2 A new worldview, which we introduce, is based on the concepts that form the foundation of our overall study of Nature as a whole. We differentiate the Cosmic Universe and also *Our* **World**, which is characterized by the **Order of Existence** of individual natural objects.

7.45.3 *Our* World is represented by the phenomena of **Origin, Motion** and **Existence**, which are explained by the *scientific theories of evolution, mechanics **and** adequate functioning*, correspondingly.

7.45.4   The new worldview does **not** negate the knowledge brought by the theories of evolution and mechanics. Rather it applies this knowledge for understanding of the *pertinent* phenomena – those belonging to the areas of Origin and Motion.

7.45.5   The new worldview uses the <u>Theory of Existence (Theory of Adequate Functioning)</u> for understanding of phenomena belonging to the *whole* area of Existence of natural objects.

7.45.6   The new worldview applies the new <u>Theory of Human Relationships</u> for understanding of *social* behavior and interactions of people.

7.45.7   Thus the <u>scientific</u> base of the new worldview is *broader* than that used now. Furthermore, the *appropriate* fundamental scientific theories –those explaining phenomena of Existence as well as phenomena of Origin and Motion are used for understanding of the ongoing events. This precludes the inevitable errors of judgement caused by misapplication of the scientific theories.

7.45.8   Knowledge upon which the new worldview is based is <u>not limited by one source</u> – science. *All* the knowledge that the humankind possesses provided by <u>different sources</u> forms the foundation of the new worldview. The role of Science was discussed above. The role of other major common sources of knowledge is analyzed below.

Alexander A. Yabrov, MD, PhD, DSc

Chapter 8.
Philosophy

8.1 Philosophy should not imitate science

8.1.1 Philosophy is an independent fundamental source of knowledge. Similar to the other sources of objective knowledge, philosophy studies Reality – which is Nature in its manifestations. Its aim is to <u>describe</u> the subject of study in ideas *(Notions)*. Its leading methods are observation, contemplation and generalization.

8.1.2 Philosophy discovers all the entire areas of nature. It differentiates them from others – the known ones, and defines them by the *new notions*. Thus philosophy answers a one of the eternal questions: *What*? What exists and what occurs with that what exists.

8.1.3 Having its task and its methods of investigation, philosophy does **not** need to imitate the tasks and methods of science. Philosophy existed and successfully fulfilled *its* tasks using *its* methods long before the modern science developed (on the basis of natural philosophy).

8.1.4 By discovering notions, philosophy *precedes* science and *shows the directions* for the scientific studies. Therefore philosophy is named the *Queen of the Sciences*. Such general notions as the universe, order, chaos, being, time, and light were developed by the method of philosophy. Natural philosophy also developed such broad notions as dynamics, change, void, atom, mass, speed, and many others. *Now science* studies the areas of phenomena *described* by the philosophical notions aiming to *explain* them using *its* methods.

8.2 Modern philosophy *follows* science instead of *leading* it.

8.2.1 Modern philosophers happened to be *bedazzled* by the Enlightenment.

8.2.2 Modern philosophy mistook the tasks of science in place of its own. It tries to imitate the method of science using mathematical logic and symbols. And formulating philosophical discourse in pseudo-mathematical formulae.

8.2.3 Today philosophy *follows* science, instead of leading it. Since the fundamental *scientific* theories do **not** explain Existence, philosophy excluded from its consideration the problems of Being as nonsensical. Meanwhile, philosophy is primarily a study of Being (Existence).

8.3 Language is merely a tool for *description* of Reality, but it is not a Reality

8.3.1   Wittgenstein and Russell developed linguistic philosophy. Language, however, is merely a *tool for description of reality*. Reality consists of objects and notions. Language is *not* a reality itself. Words are neither phenomena, nor the notions describing them – words are the symbols of the latter. Logic of words cannot and it should **not** replace logic of real life.

8.3.2   It is as easy and cheap to "experiment" with the words, as to experiment with the pebbles. A scientific experimenting with the pebbles, however, might bring some knowledge about *motion*. While philosophical experimenting with the words cannot bring any knowledge of *existence,* except some *narrow* topics related to linguistics proper. Therefore I disagree with Wittgenstein's linguistic philosophy.

8.4 A System of *Our* World

8.4.1   In our time of the prevalence of science, the philosophical system-building is deemed to be a futile activity and a matter of the past. It is suggested that the entire Universe, including *Our* World, could be explained by a general *scientific theory,* like the TOE (theory of everything). But the scientific theories describe the processes. There is **no** process that would govern *all* the natural phenomena. Therefore a *scientific* theory cannot describe Nature as a whole, which always was the task of metaphysics.

8.4.2   Aristotle characterized Metaphysics as "a science that studies being as being and the properties characteristic of it".

> In opposition to the views of the ancient philosophers, Wittgenstein in his *Tractatus* advised "...to say nothing except...propositions of natural science...and then, whenever someone else tries to say something metaphysical, to demonstrate to him that he had failed to give a meaning to certain signs in his sentences" (6.53).

8.4.3   The metaphysical systems built by the ancients served the purpose of describing the world as it was understood in *their* times.

Denying meaning to metaphysics, modern philosophy precludes any attempts to create a contemporary system describing *our* world as a *whole*. Meanwhile the description is necessary as a foundation for our worldview.

8.4.4   Table 1 (modified from *How Man Exists*, 2001) presents the system describing *Our* World as a whole.

Table 1. *The Unifying System: Fundamental Notions Describing Nature and the Processes Governing Natural Phenomena*

Characteristics	Name			Commentary
Universal *Discrete*	*Physiology of Nature*			*Nature exists by the Principle of Adequate Function via interaction of the fundamental processes.*
Fundamental Notions describing Nature	*Origin*	*Existence*	*Motion*	*All the natural phenomena are described by these fundamental notions*
Corresponding Fundamental Processes	*Evolution*	*Adequate functioning*	*Physical - chemical interaction*	*These fundamental processes govern all the natural phenomena of Our World*

8.4.5   We characterize our system as *philosophico-scientific* because it presents reality in the form of <u>notions</u> and <u>processes.</u> The notions of <u>Physiology of Nature</u> and of the <u>Principle of Adequate Function</u> serve for description of all the phenomena of *our* world. In this sense, they are *universal.* They bear an idea of Nature being organized, actively functioning, and self-supporting. Nature, thus, is not a display of the still, passive dead things and the short-lived separated living creatures scattered and lost in the uncertainty of this causeless, unpredictable world. The concept of the System conveys the view that Nature *exists* as a unified whole by actively maintaining itself trough function – adequate function, provided by all the processes and mechanisms acting continuously in concert.

8.5   The answers to the key questions

8.5.1   The scientific Theory of Existence and the Theory of Human Relationships (based on the former theory) are a part of the System. The system allows us to answer philosophical questions, which remained unanswered in spite of the efforts of thinkers during the ages:

> *What is Idea or Thing-in-itself?*
> *What is Being?*
> *What is Existence?*
> *What is moral?*
> *What is immoral?*

8.5.2   Leading philosophers believed that knowledge about an object obtained through our senses was *incomplete*. There remained an underlined unknowable part, they insisted, not amenable to our senses. Plato named it Idea or Form. Kant named it the Thing-in-itself. Not having a full knowledge about things, it was impossible to answer "What is Being".

8.5.3   The Theory of Existence explains that the part of an object that is in-amenable to our senses is underline function. It **is knowable** using the scientific methods of investigation.

8.5.4   ***Being is the unity of structure and function of an existing object***. Structure is what we know about an object via our senses. Function is what we do not perceive through senses. **Without function, there is no Being**.

8.5.5   *Existence* is a unity of structure and function *in the process of adequate (or inadequate) functioning.* **Without a process, there is no Existence.**
I would say that the notion of *Being* describes an underline object *as is* – with its structure and function. Whereas the notion of *Existence* describes a underline phenomenon – that is an object **and** what is going on with the object. The difference is similar to that between a photo and a motion picture. It is in the *dynamics* of existence.

8.5.5   Says Ayer in his *Language, Truth and Logic*:

> "We begin by admitting that the fundamental ethical concepts are unanalysable, inasmuch as there is no criterion by which one can test the validity of judgements in which they occur"(p.107, 1970).

A scientific Theory of Human Relationships discovered this *criterion*.
***Moral* behavior** is what our theory characterizes as *adequate functioning*.

Immoral *behavior* – manifestation of *inadequate functioning* (see chapter 7).

This refutes Ayer's statement that "assertions of value are not scientific but 'emotive'" (Ibid., p. 20).

8.5.7 The aforementioned questions belong to the area of Being (or to the closely related - Existence). The fact itself that the answers to these *philosophical* questions are found by a *scientific* theory proves that the thoughts of our predecessors were not senseless. These questions were a reflection of the truth that philosophy *guides* science – philosophy posed the questions, science found the explanations.

8.5.8 Problems related to Being (Existence) are eternal. Contribution of philosophy in the study of these problems promises to bring more of extremely useful knowledge.

Chapter 9.

Religion

9.1 Religion as a source of knowledge

9.1.1 Religion is a source of an *objective* knowledge (the meaning of this assertion will become clear from further analysis).

9.1.2 Knowledge provided by religion is as unique, valuable and important as that from other leading sources - science and philosophy.

9.1.3 The primary object of religion is *man and human relationships*. Most social phenomena **cannot** be studied using an experimental method because it assumes investigation under *artificial* conditions, which inevitably distort *natural* social interactions. Many social events are a result of developments that started *generations* ago. Therefore they cannot be understood based on an immediate observation. This also means that an outcome of a certain social action, or of a response to an action may manifest itself in a remote *future* - later in life of those involved, or in the following generations. Those participating in a concrete social interaction might not foresee the negative consequences of their actions. These peculiarities of the social interactions make religion a unique source of knowledge.

9.2 Uniqueness of the method of religion

9.2.1 *Method of religion* is unique. It is *most appropriate* for the study of human relationships. Religion uses long-term observation that spans through an unlimited number of generations and embraces experience of an innumerable amount of individuals of various social strata, under all the possible conditions in any situations.

9.2.2 Furthermore, this is not a passive observation of an aloof analyst. The method of religion consists of an active everyday immediate *social interaction* with the individuals who apply to the clergy for advice and relief. This vast *first-hand experience* is collated, accumulated, and transferred to the following generation.

9.2.3 Religion does **not** need to imitate the method of science. Method of a long-term observation of human relationships is unique and irreplaceable. It leads to a much more substantiated conclusions based on the facts and the long-term experience of life than an experimental method could lead to.

9.2.4　That circumstance that religion explains the facts by referring to miracles and the revelations, and bases its conclusions on faith, does not diminish the value of the conclusions. Important is the objectivity and profundity of knowledge that the source brings, rather than the way of presentation.

9.3　Religion accumulated collective experience of the humankind

9.3.1　Results of monitoring of the immediate and the remote outcomes of various human interactions, as well as of the consequences of the advice given by the clerics, compose the *collective social experience* accumulated by religion.

9.3.2　Religion embraces the *entire social experience of the humankind,* since the process of acquisition by religion of social knowledge, and its transfer trough generations is continuous and everlasting.

9.4　Rules of religious morals are believed to be the moral rules of humanity

9.4.1　Only those conclusions, which invariably lead to the outcomes helping people to improve conditions of their existence, are selected in the religious moral code. Therefore the rules of religious morals are believed to be *the* morals of humanity.

9.4.2　An opinion exists that morals idealize human relationships; that in reality, people act only in their interests, many cheat, show callousness and cruelty. Rules of morals should not be viewed as unrealistic and idealizing the human relationships. It is *moral* to follow one's interests. Their unfounded neglect is a sin. At the same time, it is moral to consider the interests of the *others*. These are rules of behavior based upon thorough analysis of the remote results of interactions of immense numbers of individuals. When followed, they lead to improvement of conditions and prolongation of existence.

9.5　The magnitude of ideas

9.5.1　The *ideas* introduced by religion – God, good, sin and evil - are colossal.

9.5.2　I consider the idea of God as the greatest of ideas. There is no other ancient or modern idea comparable by its grandiose embrace of time, space, and things. It affirms the fact of the presence of Order in nature. The idea of eternal God personifies mankind, that is eternal as long as people follow His precepts. Thus the idea of God has unifying and stabilizing social role.

9.5.3   A notion of Good summarizes the actions that help people to exist and to improve conditions.

9.5.4   The notions of Sin and Evil fulfil a very important role as the ways of moral judgement.

9.5.5   In the terms of this study, *sin* is characterized as an inadequate functioning by a perpetrator that hurts the perpetrator and (or) those with whom he interacts.

9.5.6   Evil – the inadequate functioning that results in suffering of those with whom the perpetrator does, or does not interact immediately. The scale of suffering caused by evil is broader.

9.5.7   The idea of Godly Punishment for the sinful an evil deeds is very profound. It warns that the terrible misdeeds should eventually result in the worsening of conditions or death of the perpetrator. Religion came to this conclusion through the long-term observation of the real events of life.

9.6   Position of Man in the World

9.6.1   Religion places man in the center of inhabited universe. There is nothing arrogant in it. It is only logic and just. The creature endowed with the mightiest intellectual capacities should realize one's position among other life creatures and be responsible for one's actions.

9.6.2   Guided by the sciences of Origin and Motion, man relinquished his central position and placed himself on the same footing with the other animals. This "humbleness" resulted in the loss of responsibility presumed by the position given to man by religion. As a consequence, conditions of existence of man and of other life creatures are worsening progressively.

9.7   The precepts did not loose their guiding role

9.7.1   It is not a rarity to hear from Princeton students a question why one should follow the prescriptions from a Book written 3000 years ago, which undoubtedly became obsolete?

9.7.2   Basic rules of human relationships do not change with the change of the fashions of clothes, or methods of transportation. Based on modern scientific data, I suggest that *Homo sapiens* did not change for the 100-

120 thousand years of one's existence. Hence, the rules of human relationships, in principle, remain the same today as they were described in the Book. The moral rules resulted from summarized and collated experience of more then 100 thousand years of existence of mankind did **not** become obsolete for the last several hundreds years.

9.7.3   Evaluations and conclusions developed by religion went through the objective trial of the practice of life during tens of thousands of years. This is how the rules of morals were eventually developed. The Bible represents a treasury of knowledge based upon all-embracing social experience of man accumulated throughout the time of existence of mankind; therefore it cannot become obsolete.

9.7.4   Yet, like the other sources of knowledge, religion **should** develop. According to its tradition and its major goal, only those new ideas, which help people to improve conditions of existence and prevent oppression and destruction, are compatible with the principles of religion.

9.8   The bloody history of religion

9.8.1   All said above being true, we could not disregard and dismiss the facts of a tremendous harm and destruction committed by men (and being still perpetrated now) under the banner of religion.

9.8.2   The wrongs that were done reflect the history of development of the human society, which is as complex as humans themselves are.

9.8.3   Different peoples living in different ambient and social conditions, having different customs and beliefs, developed different religions. The function of religion was the same in all cases. It instilled a common social worldview and maintained common moral rules thus unifying the society and promoting social order.

9.8.4   Knowledge of different peoples about one another was limited and distorted. Information spread with the speed of caravans. Understanding of foreign customs and beliefs was hampered by the differences in languages. These and other similar factors made people suspicious of those whose religion was different. Religion, whose mission was to protect the believers, supported these suspicions. It warned of the dangers of dealing with the heterodoxies and the infidels and of consideration of their ideas and views. As a matter of defense of the *true* beliefs, religion called to destruction of the infidels. This is the ground for religious radicalism.

9.9 Exploitation of faith for political purposes

9.9.1 Religious precepts are subjected to interpretation. The interpreters are mortals whose views and aspirations influence their exegesis. Thus the precepts are not protected from their misreading in the interests that are far from divine.

9.9.2 The rulers exploited xenophobic religious sentiments for their political purposes. The use of religious enmity was the most effective way to substantiate one's aggressive intentions and to recruit the participants for the next shady military venture. The same reason was used for redirection of the revolting momentum of the majority of citizens dissatisfied with the rulers and for the suppression of the internal opposition. It happened before and it happens now.

9.9.3 It is necessary to emphasize that those who interpret the precepts now are influenced by the modern dominant worldview (in spite of their claims to the contrary). This is demonstrated spectacularly by their ultra-revolutionary rhetoric. However, exploitation of ideas of the evolutionary-mechanistic worldview for interpretation of current human affairs does not make of a cleric-radical an advanced thinker. Rather it makes his radicalism more extreme.

9.10 Enmity is *not* ingrained in time

9.10.1 A usual argument is that enmity between fighting groups is rooted in time trough generations, therefore it is hard to expect to achieve peace now. Consider this, however. Hostility among members of some African tribes lasts for generations. But Africans who originated from these tribes live peacefully in the USA; the same refers to the Irish and to the Arabs and Jews.

9.10.2 Contrary to prevailing opinion, enmity is **not** ingrained into generations. All depends on the *existing* individuals. It is necessary to neutralize influence of those who are interested in the maintenance of the state of hostility. First of all, it is necessary to guard children from the ideas of hostility at the age when their perception is still uncritical.

9.11 Oppression of Women – another relic of the past

9.11.1 Another relic of the past is the abasing attitude to Woman. In the past, as a consequence of division of functions in the society that was determined predominantly by personal physical strength, the woman was limited in her interaction with the world. Therefore her vision was narrowed. Most remained uneducated and illiterate. Accordingly, women were not admitted to the leading professional and political positions. Their participation in social life was limited by the family duties. Among the limitations was a strict denial of the right to be involved in the religious practices on a par with man.

9.11.2　Mechanization of labor, broadening of the occupations not involving the human physical force whatsoever, and dissemination of literacy and education erased the social differences of the genders. Equipped with knowledge, women proved their efficiency in the fulfillment of any tasks of the every day life of the society.

9.11.3　Of course, the physiological differences between the genders did not disappear. These real genuine differences dictate certain functional differentiation. Women give birth – the noblest social function, which men never will be able to fulfill. This difference, however, does not diminish the woman's spiritual strength, but rather enhances it.

9.11.4　This testifies persuasively in favor of a full participation of women in all religious practices. This undoubtedly, should promote the efficacy of the dissemination of the moral message.

9.12　A sole source of knowledge is an insufficient base for a worldview

9.12.1　The bloody and oppressive manifestations of the role of religion could persist while most of the population was illiterate, the exchange of information among peoples remained limited and unreliable, and the religion of a certain people was their *sole* general source of knowledge.

9.12.2　The Theory of Human Relationships explains that a *sole* source of knowledge, be it religion or science, is unable to provide a sufficiently versatile guidance for the adequate functioning of men at the social level.

9.13　Philosophy and science originated from religion

9.13.1　Religion created a foundation for Natural Philosophy. Following the tradition of religion, philosophy retained Man as a subject of its study. At the same time, the area of inquiry broadened. Philosophy studies Nature and Man.

9.13.2　Natural Philosophy, in its turn, created foundation for modern Science. Thus Religion served as a basis for Philosophy and Science.

9.13.3   We come to the conclusion that religion is an initial source of common human knowledge that made possible other general sources of knowledge.

9.14   How to eradicate the gap between science and religion

9.14.1   On the threshold of the 21st century we observe increasing efforts to bring science and religion closer with the aim to eradicate the gap that divides them and to substantiate an acceptance of religion as a source of useful knowledge. This movement is manifested by the following two tendencies.   According to the first one, an increasing number of individual scientists declare that they believe in God.   Another manifestation of the trend is the acknowledgement that the description by the Bible of the early cosmic and earthly events are in agreement with the descriptions introduced by modern science.

9.14.2   The problem, however, is that these approaches cannot help to eradicate the divide between science and religion. That fact that some scientists are believers does not change the overall view that science is the *only* source of objective knowledge. Neither does a scientific interpretation of the creation restore the balance.   It admits that *in the light of the modern scientific theories,* religious descriptions acquire certain merit and therefore deserve attention.   Science, however, retains its dominant position of a sole source of knowledge to rely upon. The divide remains. Knowledge provided by religion and philosophy, though it is appreciated, remains unneeded and therefore unused.

9.14.3   Our analysis shows that the phenomena currently considered by science belong to the areas of *motion* and *origin*.   Religion and natural philosophy, however, consider primarily the phenomena that belong to the area of *existence*. This is where the incongruity lies. Thus I came to the conclusion that the divide that separates science from religion is not warranted: these are two sources of knowledge, which study *different subjects.*

9.14.4   Science, religion, and philosophy should have a *common* sphere of phenomena, which they consider *jointly*. The sphere of *Existence*; in particular the area of *human relationships,* is the one where religion and philosophy are the sources of thousands of years of knowledge, the reliability and usefulness of which are assured by the experience of generations.

9.14.5   To enable science to make its *useful* contribution to the knowledge provided by religion and philosophy, it is necessary to apply a new fundamental *scientific* theory – *a Theory of Existence,* and the particular social one – a *Theory of Human Relationships* based on the former. A joint study in the sphere of Existence should eradicate the gap between science and religion. A demonstrative example of harmony between science, philosophy and religion is presented in our analysis of the notion of morals, which is the case where these sources of knowledge jointly tackle a problem that belongs to the sphere of Existence (Chapter 7).

9.15 Religion and science should *collaborate* in the resolution of the problems of our existence

9.15.1 The sphere, where the collaboration of religion and science is necessary, is tremendous. As was discussed, it comprises the social problems. It also includes the problems of overpopulation, deterioration of the environment, and an increased extinction of the living creatures, all of which are tightly interwoven. As a matter of fact, overpopulation is the primary cause of a great deal of the social problems, and also of those of deterioration of the environment, and an enhanced extinction of living creatures.

9.15.2 It seems that the collaboration of the scientists with clerics and believers on the problem of overpopulation is impossible. The scientific data show that the current growth of the population exceeds the Earth's capacity to sustain ecological balance. Believers, on the other hand, insist on the Godly precept: *procreate and multiply.*

9.16 *Procreate and multiply* – this precept is fulfilled

9.16.1 Read this precept in its *completeness*:

> And God blessed Noach and his sons, and He said to them: Be fruitful and multiply and fill the earth. And your dread and your awe shall be upon all animals of the earth and on all birds of the heaven, on all that moves upon the earth and on all fish of the sea; into your hand are they given (Noach 9:1/9:2).

9.16.2 If we thoroughly analyze the current situation concerning the amount of people and their interrelation with the other living creatures, we come to a conclusion that **this precept has been fulfilled!** People did fill the Earth and they subdued the other creatures.

9.16.3 This is an entirely new situation that concerns everyone. It does not mean that somebody "won" or "lost" in an endless fruitless quarrel. Rather it means that we all should *together* decide what should we do after we did fulfill His precept.

9.16.4 There is no a simple solution. Birth rate reduction might be needed. Yet it may create a very serious problem. The ratio of the young to the old will progressively diminish. In a relatively short period, there will be insufficient amount of the young adults to support the old ones (and the children). There is a suggestion to raise the retirement age to 80. But the only way it will be practical is if the old *remain healthy*.

9.16.5 The sciences of existence: Physiology, Medicine, Biotechnology, Biology of Existence of Individual Organisms (a science different from that of Biology of Origin of Species), and Social sciences – should contribute weightily. All the above sciences are based on the general Theory of Existence.

9.17 A major aim of all religions

9.17.1 Religion promoted the spread of literacy and education. It was conducive for the development of natural philosophy and, consequently, of science and technology. The latter improved communication which promoted the exchange of ideas, which, in its turn, furthered mutual understanding among different peoples and different religions.

9.17.2 Contemporary knowledge shattered the myths of the principal differences in the humane nature of the people of different religions or races. Consequently, a general basic role of Religion became clear - *maintenance and promotion of the principles of morals.* **This is the major aim and the major function of all religions.**

9.17.3 A religion, which disseminates hatred and enmity and calls to killing, destroys the very essence and the moral sense of religious belief. Thus it destroys its own foundation.

Chapter 10.
Technology

10.1 Modern technology is based on science

10.1.1 Technology is a one of the major general sources of knowledge. It is enough to mention the new knowledge brought by the Hubble telescope, or by the Magnetic Resonance Imaging (MRI) technology.

10.1.2 Modern technology is based on science. Close interaction of these sources of knowledge results in amplification of their efficacy.

Chapter 11.

Art

11.1   Definition and the foundation

11.1.1   Art is a source of knowledge that reflects the experience and views of the artist expressed by means of a craft.
11.1.2   Art is based on all other sources of knowledge.

11.2   Art describes Existence

11.2.1   The sphere of phenomena considered and described by Art is that of *Existence*. Therefore the primary sources forming the spiritual base of Art always were *natural philosophy* and *religion* – the sources of knowledge dealing with the problems of existence.

11.3   Evolutionary-mechanistic world-view deprived Art of its spiritual base

11.3.1   With the development of the evolutionary-mechanistic worldview, the influence of philosophy and religion faded progressively. Consequently, Art was gradually *losing* its spiritual base.
11.3.2   Spiritual impoverishment of Art was reflected by the kaleidoscopic succession of the "isms".
11.3.4   In a desperate search of some general source of knowledge to rely upon, Art <u>eventually</u> found its base in *science* and *technology*.
11.3.5   Cubism, a style developed by Picasso and Braque, presents a reflection of influence of science and technology upon artistic vision. In the following works of these masters the silhouettes – whether of people, houses, or trees, even of a guitar - replaced the real objects. It can be suggested that this way the artists expressed the ideas of *relativity* and u*ncertainty*, which increasingly occupied the thoughts of the scientists. Transformed into notions of relativism and indeterminacy, these notions consequently shaped the general worldview.

11.4 Without a spiritual base, Art inevitably degrades

11.4.1 An insurmountable problem of modern Art is that science and technology *cannot* serve as its spiritual basis because science and technology, as they are practiced now, do not study phenomena of Existence. Meanwhile, *Existence is the primary subject of Art.*

11.4.2 Having no spiritual base provided by religion and philosophy, and in the absence of a scientific theory of existence, Art **lost** its soul and its creative aim.

11.5 *Shock* is not the aim of Art – it is Art's by-product

11.5.1 Picasso and Braque discovered certain new general ideas, those of relativity and uncertainty, which influenced development of the worldview at the dawn of the 20th century. These great masters also found a way to depict these new ideas. For these creative discoveries, these outstanding artists-thinkers received a deserved acclaim.

The new ideas and the ways of their presentation shocked the public. Shock as such, however, was **not** *the achievement itself* for which these masters received their recognition.

11.5.2 The claim that the task and the aim of Art are to shock is as erroneous and senseless as is to suggest that the air pollution and poisoning of the people are the task and the aim of car-making.

11.5.3 The following utterance, which is tremendously popular among modern artists, is ascribed to Marcel Duchamp:

"Unless a picture shocks, it is nothing".

Duchamp is the *author* of the "Mona Lisa" with a moustache and a goatee added. His attitude to Art and Society had led the way to Pop-art. Proceeding from the Worldview of Existence, I oppose this claim. I say:

Unless a picture has a creative, moral idea, it is nothing.

11.6 A worldview of existence should resurrect the Art

11.6.1 Guided by the currently dominant evolutionary-mechanistic worldview in the absence of an appropriate spiritual base, the contemporary popular art (pop-art) propagates ideas of relativism, immorality, nonjudgementalism, mutual hatred, and the like. The ways of expression of these ideas are: vulgar language and manners, depiction of violence, pornography, blasphemy and other similar manifestations of modernity.

11.6.2   The aim of this study is not just to list some examples of the current cultural degradation – this has been done by many. Our goal is to find and expose the *cause* of decay and suggest the ways to its *remedy*.

11.6.3   The above analysis leads us to a definitive conclusion – the <u>cause</u> of the current spiritual and moral degeneration is the dominant <u>evolutionary-mechanistic worldview,</u> which currently guides human relationships. <u>A change of the current worldview to that of **existence** should resurrect Art.</u>

Chapter 12.
General Conclusion

12.1 Behavior of human individuals differs from behavior of physical particles

12.1.1 *This study shows that the currently dominant worldview of uncertainty, rejection of causality, and preferential reliance on statistical probability is unwarranted.*

12.1.2 This view is based on conclusions drawn from the physical studies of behavior of particles. In other words, it is based on the comparatively narrow studies in the sphere of phenomena of Motion. In particular - motion and interaction of *physical particles*. Conclusions from such a narrow study should not be generalized for the explanation of *all* natural phenomena.

12.1.3 Even if we try to apply these conclusions *within* the area of Motion, but in relation to the phenomena of interaction of *physical bodies*, we find that **none** of the above conclusions remains to be valid. *Different mechanisms* are acting at these levels of organization (the electro-magnetic, and the strong and weak forces of interaction - at the level of particles; and the force of gravitation - at the level of visible bodies). And, of course, these conclusion are *not applicable* for the explanation of natural phenomena from other spheres, *besides* that of Motion, namely, those of Existence and Origin, because of the difference of both the *processes* and the *mechanisms* involved.

12.2 I explained <u>How</u> the natural objects exist

12.2.1 To explain the surrounding world, we choose to consider *Our* World – the world in which we live, *separately* from the rest of the Universe. *Our* world is characterized by Order, the basis and the manifestation of which is the *Existence* of natural objects.

12.2.2 All the phenomena of *our* world belong to those of Motion, Origin and Existence.

12.2.3 Phenomena of Motion and Origin are explained by the general theories – of mechanics (classical and quantum) and evolution, correspondingly. Phenomena that belong to the sphere of Existence (which is the broadest) remained unexplained by a general scientific theory, so far.

12.2.4 I introduced a general Theory of Existence, which discovered the *process* underlying all the phenomena of Existence - the process of <u>Adequate Functioning</u>. It acts at all the levels of organization of existing objects. Therefore we classify it as a *fundamental* process. The theory of existence described also the *mechanisms* responsible for the process of adequate functioning at different organizational levels.

12.2.5 Our study, thus, broadened the sphere of natural phenomena explained by science. **It explained *How* the natural objects *exist*.**

12.3 A <u>worldview</u> is a common idea of the majority about the World. The currently dominant evolutionary-mechanistic worldview misguides us. <u>It should be changed</u>

12.3.1 This book is centered particularly on a certain area of the phenomena of Existence, namely - *human relationships*. We study *whether* and *how* the modern science influences human relationships.

12.3.2 To answer these questions, we introduced a notion of a **WORLDVIEW**, which, in difference from the *personal* view, describes a *collective view of the majority at the world in which we live.*

12.3.3 I defended a proposition that the currently dominant worldview is based upon the scientific theories of evolution and mechanics, which represent an *inappropriate* basis for consideration and explanation of human relationships.

12.3.4 A scientific theory is able to explain *only* those phenomena, which are underlain by the process discovered by this theory. Neither the process of physical-chemical interactions, nor that of evolution underlies phenomena of Existence. Hence these theories *cannot serve as a basis* for study and understanding of human relationships.

12.3.5 Discovery of the notion of worldview and of the fact of inappropriateness of the evolutionary-mechanistic worldview for understanding of human relationships allows us to explain the state of a progressing socio-cultural degradation that takes place throughout the world currently.

12.3.6 Based upon an inappropriate scientific foundation, the currently dominant worldview *misguides* individual behavior and relationships of the citizens and hinders their efforts directed to improvement of the conditions of existence.

12.3.7 Based on our studies, we came to conclusion that *it is necessary to change the dominant worldview.*

Alexander A. Yabrov, MD, PhD, DSc

12.4 A Worldview of Existence

12.4.1   In replacement of the current evolutionary-mechanistic worldview, a *new worldview* is introduced – a **Worldview of Existence**. It is based on a new social theory – The Theory of Human Relationships, which in its turn, is founded on a general Theory of Existence.

12.4.2   At the end of the 19th century, there was an opinion that science had neared its end. The scientific discoveries that followed soon refuted this opinion. The ideas of an ending of science echoed again at the end of the 20th century. But the flow of new discoveries did not cease. A scientific explanation of an entirely different area of natural phenomena presented in this *Tractatus* is a one more proof that science is far from being exhausted.

12.4.3   The new worldview does *not* negate the knowledge provided by the theories of evolution and mechanics. Rather it uses it *where it belongs*: for the explanation of phenomena of Origin and Motion. Meanwhile, the phenomena of Existence are explained by the theories of existence and of the human relationships.

12.4.4   Thus the *scientific* base of the new worldview is *broader*. It includes knowledge provided by the fundamental theories of evolution and mechanics (classical and quantum) *and* by the theory of adequate functioning (the theory of Existence).

12.4.5   This is **not** all – the new worldview also employs knowledge provided by *other* general sources, including Philosophy, Religion and Art.

12.4.6   Based on the new worldview, we might expect a **renaissance** in all the areas of knowledge related to the sphere of phenomena of Existence including philosophy, religion, arts, medicine, biology, and the social sciences.

12.4.7   Knowledge provided by the Worldview of Existence allows us to understand the laws by which Man exists. It discovers the process and the mechanisms governing human relationships directed toward improvement of conditions of existence. This understanding should help us to stop and reverse the process of socio-cultural decay that threatens the very existence of humankind.

12.4.8   Taking into account a crucial influence of a worldview on human relationships, it is necessary that the new worldview be *actively implemented*. The media, the educators, and the educated should play a decisive active role in the process of dissemination of the new knowledge.

12.5 Philosophy is the Queen of Sciences

12.5.1 Being a philosopher, Wittgenstein could allow himself to keep a mystery. Furthermore, this is a mystery that maintains the keen interest to his *Tractatus* for almost a century. A scientist could **not** allow the study remain mystical. Clarity of understanding and of explanation is demanded from a scientific study. If achieved, it should maintain the interest of the readers.

12.5.2 Said Wittgenstein:

> "My propositions serve as elucidations in the following way: anyone who understands me eventually recognizes them as nonsensical, when he has used them – as steps – to climb up beyond them. (He must, so to speak, throw away the ladder he has climbed up it). He must transcend these propositions, and then he will see the world aright" (6.54).

I suggest that Wittgenstein is undeservedly too critical of his work. I do not perceive his propositions as nonsensical. I believe that Wittgenstein *saw* phenomena of Existence, but had difficulty in describing, let alone explaining them. Being limited by the evolutionary-mechanistic worldview, he "knew" that this "metaphysics" was just a linguistic error. I changed the term "nonsensical" to that of "Existence" and discovered the world aright. This demonstrates again that philosophy precedes science. It shows a direction for the scientific studies. Philosophy *is* the Queen of Sciences. Yet a principal difference in the worldviews exists: Wittgenstein's *Tractatus* promulgated ideas of uncertainty and chaos. Whereas the *Tractatus*, which you have read, instills the ideas of Reliability and Order of Reason, Morals and Law on a global scale.

Alexander A. Yabrov, MD, PhD, DSc

Epilogue

Twenty years ago, when I just started to put these ideas in a coherent form, I had sent a brief compendium to Sir Karl Popper and to Professor James Watson[3]. Sir Karl, a philosopher, did not have doubts about the necessity of the study. His support during many years played decisive role in the success of my work. The response of Dr. Watson was also positive. He found that the work had certain merits and gave it for review to the two of his senior scientists. I had a telephone conversation with one of them, whose personal opinion was highly favorable. The other reviewer was a head of the Virology Laboratory. She asked: **"What is it for?"**

Being a Ph.D. in Medical Virology myself, I understand clearly the above straightforward question. From a specific professional viewpoint of a virologist whose concern is human health, it is not obvious, whether a scientific-philosophical synthesis is needed. Let alone the synthesis of human knowledge from *all* major sources – experience, science, philosophy, religion, technology, and art. All this is just "philosophy" – a derogatory remark.

The reader will be the judge.

The essence of this scientifico-philosophical study is the following.

It analyses the common Western view at the World in which we live and characterizes it as the evolutionary-mechanistic one. It discovers that this worldview is based on the scientific theories, which, though correct, nevertheless **do not** and **cannot** explain how man *exists*.

Further it discovers that this worldview essentially influences behavior and relationships of the people in a misleading way. This *Tractatus* qualifies the misguiding influence of the dominant worldview as the major cause of the currently observed social degradation.

The study introduces a *new* – broader - *worldview* – the **Worldview of Existence**. It allocates the influence of the theories of evolution and mechanics where it is appropriate, namely, to the areas of phenomena of Origin and Motion. It introduces a new general Theory of Existence and a based on it Theory of Human Relationships. These theories form the scientific basis for our understanding of phenomena of existence in general, and of existence of man, in particular. Still *in addition* to the above, the knowledge provided by *other*

---

[3] James Watson was awarded the 1962 Nobel Prize for discovery of structure of DNA.

sources, such as *philosophy, religion* and *art*, is employed for understanding of the human relationships.

Of course, the problems of our physical health are important. But the problems of our *social health* are not less important for everyone. And besides, the general theory of existence and the corresponding worldview serve as a reliable description of reality and a scientific basis for all the *Sciences of Existence*, to which I refer Physiology and Medicine, Biotechnology, Biology of Existence of Individual Organisms (in difference from the Biology of Origin of Species), and the Social Sciences. Existence is the central area of phenomena of *Our* World. I exert all my efforts to promote development of *all* the Sciences of Existence.

Index

Alexander A. Yabrov, MD, PhD, DSc

Author of the Foreword.

Dr. David Horrobin obtained medical and neuroscience degrees from Oxford and became a Fellow of Magdalen College. He helped to found the University of Nairobi Medical School in Kenya; headed experimental Laboratories and taught at the universities of London, Newcastle and Montreal. His multifarious studies resulted in development of an academic school in a very complex area of biochemistry and pathophysiology, viz., metabolism of essential fatty acids. The voluminous studies of this school contributed tremendously to our understanding of the mechanisms of action of prostaglandins and leukotriens – natural bioactive substances playing key role in cell regulation, immunity, inflammation, and other functions of the human organism. Dr. Horrobin's creative work represents a harmonic unity of original theoretical generalizations and thorough experimental and clinical investigations. He is an author of a theory discovering a general mechanism of such seemingly disparate severe diseases as schizophrenia, rheumatoid arthritis, diabetic neuritis, and some other chronic illnesses. Dr. Horrobin allocates a great deal of efforts to the practical application of basic science to medicine. His basic studies and the results of their clinical application are described in his pioneering books "Prostaglandins" (1978) and "Omega-6" (1990) and in over 400 papers, particularly in the fields of neuroscience and psychiatry. His scientific investigations contributed essentially to the development of science in different countries. Dr. Horrobin has conducted medical research projects in the Himalayas and in Africa as well as Europe and North America. Vast sphere of his creative activity also includes intensive promotion of development of new ideas in medicine. Dr. Horrobin is a founding editor of two international scientific journals: "Medical Hypotheses" and "Prostaglandins and Leukotriens". Founded with the help of Sir Karl Popper and Nobel Laureates John Eccles, Macfarlane Burnet and Linus Pauling, "Medical Hypotheses" represents a forum for discussion of the innovative original concepts in the area of health and disease far greater in the breadth of its scope than any other area of science.

About the Author

The unique life history undoubtedly prepared this author for the discovery of a fundamental scientific Theory of Existence (*How Man Exists*, 2001) and, based on it, for the concept of a w*orldview of existence* described in the *Tractatus*.

Dr. Yabrov was born in Leningrad (now St. Petersburg), in the family of educated proletarians. His mother was a weaver who became a textile engineer. Father was a metallurgical worker and a student of a mechanical institute when he was arrested, in 1937, as millions of other innocent people were. The arrest took place in presence of his six-year old son. Vividly remembering this scene, Alexander made a conscious decision never to become a member and accomplice of the Young Communist Union and of the Communist Party. Since the former was obligatory for every 13 old, Alex, not asking anybody for an advice, developed an elaborate plan to validate his objection. He created situations where he would be forced to fight with the older students. Each time when the activists approached him insisting on his membership, he parried with the reply that he did not deserve the honor, because he could not control his instincts. This experience eventually brought him the 2nd place in the Leningrad boxing championship. He was also a qualified mountain climber (Caucasus). This was the way he trained his character for the exploration and surmounting of the heights of science and philosophy that loomed ahead. Meanwhile, from the labor camp, his father advised him to leave the school and become an electrical welder – a profession, which he might use in Gulag when his turn would come. But he finished the school with an academic medal and entered the medical institute. Doctors were also needed in the camps. For several years he treated children and adults sick with various severe infectious diseases at the northern border. This first hand clinical (and social) experience helped Doctor Yabrov to always see the real patient through the wall of an experimental test-tube when he later became a scientist-experimenter - medical virologist and cell biologist. However, at first it was necessary to overcome the social barriers. His starting social credentials did not promise any possibility for career advancement. Not a Party member, but a member of a persecuted minority. Father – a former political prisoner (was exonerated and returned after 18 years, when his 6-year old son became a doctor and a father himself). Yet, perseverance and the will to become a scientist allowed Dr. Yabrov to enter a graduate course at the Department of Virology of the Institute of Experimental Medicine of the USSR Academy of Medical Sciences. He organized and headed for 10 years a Laboratory studying and manufacturing vaccines against influenza, polio, encephalitis, and diphtheria. His scientific interests were centered on the mechanisms of resistance of the organism, especially the so-called nonspecific mechanisms, whose nature and function were less understood. These investigations were performed primarily on the molecular and cellular levels. Dr. Yabrov introduced an idea that a human cell should be considered as an organism in itself. He differentiated the system of cellular mechanisms as those regulatory, compensatory and defense, each providing for existence and resistance of the cells. These studies, having general biological scope, were beyond the narrow themes developed in the Virology Department of the Medical Academy. Dr. Yabrov became an acknowledged expert in a new area – cellular mechanisms of resistance. From the position of a Senior Scientist of the Academy of Medical Sciences he was elected as a Senior Scientist of the USSR Academy of Sciences of the Radiobiology Department, Leningrad Nuclear Physics Institute. At the Academy, he organized and headed for 7 years the inter-institutional, interdisciplinary studies of the cellular mechanisms of resistance. These studies produced a conclusion that the cell has mechanisms protecting its vital structures-functions, such as the genome, protein synthesis, energy and transport. Hence, it is necessary to look for the mechanisms of resistance not according to the specific interests of the investigators, e.g., against some bacteria, or viruses, or radiation, but rather according to the vital interests of the cell itself. These cellular mechanisms Dr. Yabrov classified as the *mechanisms of security*. (This original direction of studies prompted a keen interest of the US Office of Homeland Security – described in the *Tractatus*). In 1973, Dr. Yabrov applied for an emigration visa. This was a very risky decision considering his position, from which he voluntarily resigned. After a very tense year of an uncertainty and grave danger, he and the family were free. During 1.5 year in Israel, Dr. Yabrov organized a clinical laboratory in Rehovot. This laboratory, where children are treated with interferon, is still functioning. In 1976, he moved to Canada. In Toronto, he performed experimental studies on cancer. He also had written a book on interferon, which was awarded as the Best Book of the Year (see further).

Since 1979, Dr. Yabrov has worked in the United States as Director of Research and Development of the National Patent Development Corporation, New York, NY – New Brunswick, NJ. First in the US, he organized the production of interferon on an industrial scale for clinical purposes. The initial studies on the anti-cancer effect of interferon approved by the FDA were performed using interferon produced by Dr. Yabrov. From 1980 to 1990, he held a position of a visiting research professor at Rutgers – the State University of New Jersey. Several major directions of studies should be mentioned. The first concerns the development of medicine in the era of prevalence of chronic diseases in the long-living society – a direction defined and substantiated by Dr. Yabrov based on his long-term observations. Here the idea of a cell being an organism played a pivotal role. As an organism, a human cell fulfils a dual function: it satisfies its own needs and also the needs of the organism. A balance of these functions provides for health; the imbalance is prone to disease. These studies led to discovery of a general mechanism of chronic diseases, and development of a modern theory of pathology. Thorough observations in the areas of medicine and biology led Dr. Yabrov toward an entirely new and much broader direction of studies, which resulted in a discovery of a new sphere of natural phenomena – those of Existence. Unexpectedly, it was found that the major area of natural phenomena did not have a general scientific explanation. During more then 10 years Dr. Yabrov worked on a scientific theory of Existence. This new general theory is described in his recent monograph How Man Exists.

Currently, Dr. Yabrov is a President of a research company in Princeton, NJ. The applied studies in the US, besides interferon, include those on the new methods of transmission of information to and within the organism, and also new methods of prevention and treatment of mental retardation and learning disabilities.

Over a 100 scientific publications. Ten patents.

Monographs:

Interferon and Nonspecific Resistance (1980) – The Best Book of the Year 198
in Health Area (Awarded by the American Publishers Association).
How Man Exists (2001).
From Uncertainty of Ignorance to Uncertainty of Science. Tractatus Scientific
Philosophicus (to be published, 2002).

In preparation:

Direct Computer-Organism Interaction. Medicine without Drugs.
A Challenge to Physicists.
AMERICA - Strength and Weaknesses.

Besides these primarily basic theoretical works, Dr. Yabrov has developed a line
of experimental projects of applied character, in particular - an absolutely
original Project of prophylactics and treatment of cancer. This 2 to 3 year project
is based on the results of his long-term experimental studies. The work on the
project should start as soon as the sufficient funding is obtained.

The above brief description demonstrates the uniqueness and the breadth of
scope of experience and expertise of the author of the Tractatus. For dozens of
years, Dr. Yabrov had experienced the political conditions of a dictatorship. For
many years he has been living now in a free world. He was a citizen of four
countries with different political systems. In each of these countries Dr. Yabrov
put all his efforts and abilities to improve conditions of existence of his fellow
citizens – sick and healthy. These efforts resulted in essential useful
contributions. This Tractatus is one of these contributions, whose creative
beneficial influence will be manifested over the borders that divide us. Among
other things, a new worldview developed by the Tractatus should help to
eradicate radicalism, which creates the basis for terrorism.